THE BEGGAR'S OPERA

BEGGAR'S OPERA, ACT III
"When my hero in court appears"

THE

BEGGAR'S OPERA

BY

John Gay

With an Introduction by Oswald Doughty

29 Illustrations

DOVER PUBLICATIONS, INC.
NEW YORK

Published in Canada by General Publishing
Company, Ltd., 30 Lesmill Road, Don Mills,
Toronto, Ontario.
Published in the United Kingdom by Constable
and Company, Ltd., 10 Orange Street, London WC 2.

This Dover edition, first published in 1973, is an
unabridged and unaltered republication of the
edition published by Daniel O'Connor, London,
1922. The present edition contains a new supple-
ment, "The Music for the Overture and the Songs
in The Beggar's Opera," reproduced from the
original 1729 edition.

International Standard Book Number: 0-486-22920-3
Library of Congress Catalog Card Number: 72-96623

Manufactured in the United States of America
Dover Publications, Inc.
180 Varick Street
New York, N. Y. 10014

CONTENTS

LIST OF ILLUSTRATIONS

EDITOR'S INTRODUCTION

Nos haec novimus esse nihil.[1]

SO runs the modest epigraph which Gay prefixed to his *Beggar's Opera* in 1728; but in this the world did not agree with him, and it was well for Gay that it did not. It was, indeed, as possible in the early Eighteenth Century as it is to-day for the uncritical enthusiasm of popular opinion to bring fame and fortune to a hitherto obscure and still undeserving writer. But when in the year 1728 the English public took John Gay to its unfathomable heart, it might, if called to account, have furnished reasons for its action better than any it could have produced on some similar but more recent occasions.

For, long before this, John Gay (1685-1732), the former silk-mercer's apprentice, had become conspicuous as a writer of poems and plays. He was already the intimate friend and companion of the literary leaders of the age, Pope and Swift, and had found aristocratic friends and protectors in the beautiful and influential Duchess of Queensberry and her husband. Gay's *Fables*, which had appeared in the preceding year, 1727, were now winning for him a reputation greater than that acquired by means of *Wine, Rural Sports, The Shepherd's Week, Trivia*, or any other of his previous works.

But appreciation, even of his *Fables*, was restricted to the reading section of the public, and literary fame, though increasing, was comparatively slow. With the appearance of *The Beggar's Opera*, however, Gay found greatness thrust upon him. Fame came to him literally in a night, and Gay, like a wise man, was far from deprecating, much less rejecting, the unexpected or undeserved favours of the gods.

The Beggar's Opera is the happy resultant of a number of influences then operative upon the mind and life of the poet, and several of these are worthy of detailed examination, for

[1] 'We know that this is nothing.'

ix

the opera is not to be fully explained by the character of Gay alone. In the first place, the contemporary political situation and its effect upon Gay's life and material prospects, giving as it does the clue to the writer's mood and to the utterances of the various characters, and explaining the applause with which the public greeted them, must be considered. Secondly, the popularity of Italian opera in England at that time deserves notice, as it influenced Gay in his choice of the form in which he decided to express his feelings and to make his appeal. Finally, the general spirit of the work must be placed in relation to the collective moral and philosophic outlook (or perhaps pose) of the age, as only thus can the full significance of the play be realized, and the admiration it excited be understood. To these aspects of *The Beggar's Opera*, therefore, we now turn.

I. When on 11 June 1727 George I died, and the former Prince of Wales reigned in his stead as George II, John Gay, who, disappointed by the neglect of George I, had assiduously cultivated the patronage of the Prince and of his mistress, Mrs. Howard, not unnaturally hoped for better days. In 1720 the poet's fortunes, impaired by enormous losses in the bursting of the South Sea Bubble, had sunk to a low ebb, and now in his early forties Gay hoped for an assured position of material ease and social dignity at court.

A mistress may sway the mind of a prince, but a king should give ear to his queen alone. It was not the teaching of history, but, unfortunately for Gay, it was the opinion of George II. Mrs. Howard was powerless to help, or pretended to be so. The Queen advised, Walpole remained in power, and Gay was offered nothing more alluring than the post of 'gentleman-usher' to the Princess Louisa at a salary of about £200 a year. The post was probably a sinecure, but Gay indignantly rejected it on the plea of age.[1] Once again the Fates had betrayed him. This *annus mirabilis* of the old king's

---

[1] Pope's *Works*, ed. Elwin and Courthope, VII, 103. Underhill states that the salary was £150 but gives no authority for the statement. Lord Chesterfield says it was £200 (see Chesterfield's *Letters*, II, 441). Coxe says it was 'above £200 a year.' *Memoir of Sir Robert Walpole*, I, 279.

death, this year for which he had long waited, and which he
had freighted with such high hopes, saw him an outcast amid
the wreckage of his ambitious schemes. What wonder if, for
a time at least, the once genial poet turned cynic? What
wonder that, having suffered a double betrayal, Gay lost his
faith in humanity and sought refuge in a stoicism of despair?
The travail of his soul finds expression in a letter to Swift
written on 22 October 1727:

> As I am used to disappointments I can bear them; but as I can have
> no more hopes, I can no more be disappointed, so that I am in a blessed
> condition.[1]

Hope had died. And Walpole, who in 1722 had granted him
a beggarly commissionership of lotteries worth a mere £150 a
year, was still in office. The time was obviously out of joint,
and to Gay it was equally obvious that he was the man born
to set it right. So he turned 'agin the government,' leading
the forces of moral and political virtue against the venal
Walpole and his bribed and corrupted followers—a second
Cato, vindicating national integrity. True, he retained the
salaried post that Walpole had given him long before, but
Gay was not the man to frustrate the one good action of an
evil government. His play was begun before the dubious
honour of instructing the Princess Louisa had been offered to
him and rejected, and the letter which informed Swift of
hopes abandoned also records the completion of the play.
Throughout, Swift lurks in the background. To Swift we owe
the inception of the opera. For although Pope told Spence,
and probably with truth, that the play was written by Gay
alone,[2] the dark genius of Swift lies behind it, veiled but not
invisible, and beyond the dancing and singing puppets of the
stage, a keen eye may detect the sardonic smile of the Dean.

On 9 April 1727 Swift arrived in England, and, as a fellow
guest with Gay at Pope's Twickenham villa, witnessed the
political excitement, the heartburnings and rivalries which
attended the death of the old king and the advent of his successor. It was at this time[3] that in a conversation with Gay,

---

[1] Pope's *Works*, ed. Elwin and Courthope, VII, 103.
[2] Spence's *Anecdotes*, pp. 109-10, 120. See below, p. xxix, Appendix, Note I (*b*),(*c*).
[3] See below, p. xxix, Appendix, Note I.

Swift revived a suggestion made eleven years before,[1] remarking 'what an odd, pretty sort of thing a Newgate Pastoral might make.'[2] There was possibly some irony in the remark, but Gay was then in the mood to welcome irony, torn by the battling hopes and fears which only the king's death could lay to rest. He thought over the suggestion, and decided to make a serious attempt to put it into practice, despite the disapproval of Swift, who obviously hardly expected to be taken at his word.[3] The train of Gay's thought is obvious. Tormented by doubts of the future, his mind dwelt incessantly upon the intrigues of his enemies, 'Walpole and his gang,' as Gay must often have thought of them. They were no better than common highwaymen and pickpockets. Newgate, not the court, was the proper place for such rogues.[4] The thought of Newgate recalled Swift's remark. What had Swift said the other day? Oh yes! That a Newgate pastoral might make an odd, pretty sort of thing. Perhaps there was something in it. It had amused him at the time. How like Swift it was to make such a remark; to link Newgate, grim and ghastly, almost an English Bastille, with the simple, innocent delights of pastoral verse. And then, no doubt, Gay recalled how, only two years previously, Allan Ramsay had produced his pastoral drama, *The Gentle Shepherd*, which had been a success. To put Walpole and his friends into Newgate in a ballad-opera, now that the town was already deserting the Italian opera which had caused so much dispute, would be a fitting revenge, and better still, possibly a profitable one too. It was high time that these people were shown to the public as they really were, in their true light as robbers, who by their bribery and corruption were reducing the people to beggary. What, indeed, was Gay himself, with money gone and no snug place at court, but a beggar? It should be *The Beggar's Opera*.

It was with such thoughts as these stirring him to action,

---

[1] Swift's *Correspondence*, II, 330.
[2] Spence's *Anecdotes*, p. 120.   [3] *Ibid.*, p. 120.
[4] *Cf.* Gay's remark in a letter to Mrs. Howard, directed against Walpole and written in August 1723: 'I cannot indeed wonder that the talents requisite for a great statesman are so scarce in the world, since so many of those who possess them are every month cut off in the prime of their age at the Old Bailey.' *Suffolk Letters*, I, 118-9.

that Gay set about his task. He was not the man lightly to provoke a conflict with authority,[1] and with the immediate future so uncertain he must carefully pick his way. But he was clever enough to see that by exercising a certain dexterity of allusion he might derive profit from the adventure, whatever the result to himself of the king's death. So in moments of doubt or despair Gay saw in his play the last defiant challenge of an undaunted though beaten man. And in his more frequently prevailing mood of hopeful expectancy, he saw in it the scornful parody of a foe once powerful but now overthrown. For at such times, painting the future in the rosy colours of his desire, he saw himself transported to those seats of the mighty, from which Walpole had in his imagination been cast down. If that dream were realized, the defeat of his enemies would by this play become doubly bitter, for they must make their exit from the political stage amid the scornful laughter of the town.[2]

And over all, sustaining him in his task, was the influence of Swift, his fellow guest at Twickenham. Throughout that short summer of 1727 the three friends, Pope, Swift, and Gay, worked together at their own separate tasks, each stimulated by the proximity of the others. But the close of that Indian summer saw the close of the short Indian summer of Swift's own life. News of the failing health of Stella, now near to death, called Swift back to Ireland. So with the falling leaves of autumn about him, he took the road, and passed for ever out of the circle of distinguished friends, whose companionship had brought him what little of joy life had to give.

Solitary, in pain of mind and body, dreading the desolation of the empty home to which he was returning, dreading above all the utter loneliness which must beset him with Stella's death, Swift, delayed by contrary winds, remained for a week at Holyhead, impatiently awaiting a lull in the storm, which should allow the ship to proceed. One attempt to cross failed, and, cooped up in his smoky, unkempt room at the comfortless

[1] 'Gay was remarkable for an unwillingness to offend the great by any of his writings: he had an uncommon timidity upon him, in relation to anything of that sort.' Spence's *Anecdotes*, p. 120.
[2] See Croker's note, Pope's *Works*, ed. Elwin and Courthope, VII, 117.

village inn, unable to sleep, without books, he seeks distraction in writing to an imaginary correspondent; fills a small notebook with commonplaces, trivialities, to preserve his sanity; but ever and anon the passion of his fevered spirit breaks through. In broken dreams the friends he has left return to him; but on one theme he is silent; indomitable still, he writes:

I shall say nothing upon the suspense I am in about my dearest friend.[1]

And finally, ' peace ':

I have now not spirit enough left me to fret.[2]

Verses, too, he wrote, and once in these his ever-present sorrow finds words: characteristically, with no embroidery of sentiment:

> Before, I always found the wind
> To me was most malicious kind,
> But now the danger of a friend,
> On whom my fears and hopes depend,
> Absent from whom all Climes are curst,
> With whom I'm happy in the worst,
> With rage impatient makes me wait
> A passage to the Land I hate.[3]

And while Swift at Holyhead throughout that wild week of autumn, with its wind and rain, battled with a madness of despair, away in the south at Twickenham the friend he had left was putting the finishing touches to the work which owed its existence to the suggestion of the Dean. For Gay's opera was nearly finished, and its dainty porcelain figures were coming to life. The bright eyes of Polly were upon him, and fair, frail forms danced about him singing:

> Youth 's the Season made for Joys,
>   Love is then our Duty.

So that on 22 October Gay could write to Swift:

> My Opera is already finished.[4]

---

[1] *Life of Swift*, II, 325.   [2] *Ibid.*, II, 329.
[3] *Ibid.*, II, 320.   [4] Swift's *Correspondence*, III, 427.

Swift replied to Gay in a letter dated 23 November, wishing the poet all success in his enterprise.[1] Pope, in a letter to Swift written in January 1728, announced the approaching presentation of the play, and expressed the anxiety of Congreve and of himself as to its success:

> Whether it succeeds or not, it will make a great noise, but whether of claps or hisses I know not. At worst, it is in its own nature a thing which he can lose no reputation by, as he lays none upon it.[2]

At first, among Gay's friends, doubt was general. Pope, referring to Swift and himself, told Spence that:

> When it was done, neither of us thought it would succeed. We showed it to Congreve, who, after reading it over, said, 'It would either take greatly, or be damned confoundedly.'[3]

The Duke of Queensberry when first shown the play, delivered himself of the following discreet criticism:

> This is a very odd thing, Gay; I am satisfied that it is either a very good thing or a very bad thing.[4]

Cibber, the manager of Drury Lane, to whom the play was first offered, rejected it.[5] Rich, however, the manager of Lincoln's Inn Fields Theatre, accepted the MS., and the opera was presented for the first time on 29 January 1728.[6]

But even after acceptance, Gay's difficulties were not at an end. There was the usual trouble with the actors. Quin, after a short trial, threw up his part of Macheath,[7] and handed it over to Walker, who, though no singer, thereby 'established his reputation.'[8] On the first night Gay and his friends awaited the event in great anxiety. A remark of the Duke of Argyll,

---

[1] Swift's *Correspondence*, III, 432. [2] *Ibid.*, IV, 5.
[3] Spence's *Anecdotes*, p. 120. [4] Boswell's *Life of Johnson*, II, 368.
[5] Johnson's *Lives of the Poets*, II, 275.
[6] *The Daily Journal*, Thursday, 1 February 1728.
[7] Different reasons are given for Quin's action. Genest says it was 'from despair of acquitting himself with the dissolute gaiety and bold vigour of deportment necessary to the character.' *Some Account of the English Stage*, III, 221. Boswell, however, states that 'Quin himself had so bad an opinion of it, that he refused the part of Captain Macheath, and gave it to Walker.' Boswell's *Life of Johnson*, II, 368-9.
[8] *Some Account of the English Stage*, III, 221.

who sat in the next box, and was regarded as an authority on such matters, greatly cheered them:

It will do—it must do!—I see it in the eyes of them.[1]

At first the audience was as critical as were the fortunes of the play, until Lavinia Fenton, as Polly, by her rendering of:

O ponder well! be not severe;

captured the affections of the Duke of Bolton,[2] and the enthusiasm of the audience.[3] Thus, with growing warmth and increasing interest, the ' house ' followed the performance, until at the close its delight found vent in clamorous applause.[4]

Thus the success of the play was assured, and its fame quickly spread over the town. Pope, in a note to *The Dunciad*, witnesses to its far-reaching popularity. Songs from the play were reproduced on ladies' fans and on the screens of their drawing-rooms, and pictures of Polly, Macheath, Gay, and the rest were made and sold in large numbers.[5] Gay wrote to Swift in high glee on 15 February, describing the sustained enthusiasm of a public which nightly crowded the playhouse in Lincoln's Inn Fields.[6] On the twenty-first night the King, Queen, and princesses were present.[7]

Within a month of its appearance in London, Swift had bought a copy in an Irish edition in Dublin, where it was first acted before the end of March, amid scenes of enthusiasm equal to those it had evoked in London itself.[8] Pope, in the note to *The Dunciad*, to which reference has been made, tells us that the play

spread into all the great towns of England, was played in many places to the thirtieth and fortieth time, at Bath and Bristol fifty, etc. It made its progress into Wales, Scotland, and Ireland, where it was performed twenty-four days together. It was last acted in Minorca.[9]

---

[1] Spence's *Anecdotes*, p. 120.
[2] Pope's *Works*, ed. Warton, 1797, IX, 100 *n.*
[3] Boswell's *Life of Johnson*, II, 368.   [4] Spence's *Anecdotes*, p. 120.
[5] See note to *The Dunciad*, Book III, l. 330 ; Swift's *Correspondence*, IV, 16, 33.
[6] Swift's *Correspondence*, IV, 10. See also *ibid.*, IV, 15-6.
[7] *Notes and Queries*, 1st Series, I, 179.
[8] Swift's *Correspondence*, IV, 20-1 ; V, 220, note 1.
[9] Pope's *Works*, IV, 184, note 2.

SIR ROBERT WALPOLE

LADY CATHERINE HYDE, DUCHESS OF QUEENSBURY

In the same note Pope tells us 'It was acted in London sixty-three days uninterrupted,' but as a matter of fact it ran for sixty-two nights, thirty-two of which were in succession, and when withdrawn was attracting even larger audiences than before.[1]

Such a triumph naturally brought to Gay material rewards, not less welcome than popularity and fame.

In his first letter to Swift telling of the success of the play, Gay estimated his probable profit at 'between six and seven hundred pounds.'[2] Later, on 20 March, Gay wrote to Swift:

I have got by all this success, between seven and eight hundred pounds, and Rich, deducting the whole charge of the house, hath cleared already near four thousand pounds.[3]

Hence the wits of the time described *The Beggar's Opera* as the play which made 'Gay rich and Rich gay.'[4]

But the author's prosperity was not to remain long unchallenged. The political appeal of the opera, its ironical characterization of the chief politicians in power, above all of Walpole, delighted the many opponents of the government.

We hear a million of stories about the opera, of the encore at the song, 'That was levell'd at me,'[5] when two great Ministers were in a box together, and all the world staring at them.

So wrote Swift to Gay on 28 March 1728.[6] But the supporters of the government were placed in a difficult position by Gay's adroit handling of his material. They could not, without a confession of guilt, take him to task for caricaturing them as rogues and vagabonds. As they speedily saw, there was only

[1] See Rich's account-book, *Notes and Queries*, 1st Series, I, 178-9.
[2] Swift's *Correspondence*, IV, 10.
[3] *Ibid.*, IV, 16. See also *ibid.*, IV, 18: Gay received £693 13s. 6d. from Rich, and also sold the copyright of the opera which was printed 14 February 1728 for 90 guineas. See *Notes and Queries*, 1st Series, I, 178-9, and *Monthly Chronicle*.
[4] Johnson's *Lives of the Poets*, II, 275.
[5] See below, p. 49: 'When you censure the Age,' etc.
[6] Swift's *Correspondence*, IV, 21. That Gay's main motive was political, that it had been carefully considered and discussed by the friends at Twickenham, is clear from their writings. See Swift's *Correspondence*, IV, 12, 21, and Swift's *Works*, 1824, IX, 93-7. 'The two ministers were Walpole and Townshend.' Johnson's *Lives of the Poets*, II, 279, note 1.

one way in which Gay might be checkmated. He had come forward ostensibly as the champion of public virtue; but his opera might be represented or misrepresented, as an incitement to public vice. By accusing this popular champion of morality of having written an immoral play, they might turn the tables upon their opponent. If political morality had suddenly become Gay's chief care, the supporters of Walpole manifested with an equally immediate and suspicious enthusiasm, a zeal for the welfare of public morals, hitherto unknown. To accuse a political opponent of injuring the cause of virtue by his writings, was an old political trick which had been employed two years before, and with success, against the works of the deceased poet Prior.[1] Why should it not be equally successful when applied to Gay? Besides, the influence of the Puritans was not extinct, and there were many who were sincerely disgusted by Macheath and his gang, and believed that the influence of the play must be harmful to society. Among these the government hoped to find allies, possibly to make political converts. Thus it was that shortly after the first performance of the opera Dr. Thomas Herring, court-chaplain, and later successively Archbishop of York and of Canterbury, in a sermon at the chapel of Lincoln's Inn, denounced the play as immoral and provocative of crime.[2] Gay referred to Dr. Herring's sermon in a letter to Swift,[3] and Swift defended his friend in the *Intelligencer*, attacking the moral Herring with the remark that *The Beggar's Opera* would ' probably do more good than a thousand sermons of so stupid, so injudicious, and so prostitute a divine.'[4]

The controversy so lightly begun, was, however, taken seriously by many who followed, and throughout the century the morality of Gay's play was a frequent subject of debate. At each reappearance of the opera, the more timid supporters of public morals trembled anew. Johnson defended the play

---

[1] Wright's *Caricature History of the Georges*, pp. 69-70.

[2] See Mist's *Weekly Journal*, 30 March 1728; *Letters from Dr. Herring to Wm. Duncombe*, London, 1777, p. 3, note, and Appendix; *Seven Sermons by Dr. Herring*, London, 1763, Preface, pp. v-xvi; also *London Journal*, 30 March and 20 April 1728.

[3] Swift's *Correspondence*, IV, 33.

[4] Swift's *Works*, IX, 96.

but admitted some grounds for fear.[1] Boswell differed, seeing in it real dangers,[2] and indeed so great was his interest in the matter, that he planned to write a book on the question, and made several visits to Newgate for the purpose, but his design was frustrated by his death.[3] Boswell records a discussion he witnessed at a club, in which

A very eminent physician . . . remarked that a lively young man, fond of pleasure, and without money, would hardly resist a solicitation from his mistress to go upon the highway, immediately after being present at the representation of *The Beggar's Opera*.

Boswell also records a remark of Gibbon, that

'*The Beggar's Opera* may, perhaps, have sometimes increased the number of highwaymen; but that it has had a beneficial effect in refining that class of men, making them less ferocious, more polite, in short, more like gentlemen.' ' Upon this,' adds Boswell, ' Mr. Courtenay said, that " Gay was the Orpheus of highwaymen." ' [4]

A revival of the play at Drury Lane and Covent Garden in 1773, under the direction of Garrick and Colman respectively, led to a protest from Sir John Fielding, the Bow Street magistrate, who, fearing its influence, requested a change of programme. Garrick paid some heed to the request, but Colman returned an insolent reply,[5] while Horace Walpole, the cynic of Strawberry Hill, sarcastically described the incident in a letter to Horace Mann.[6] John Whiston, the bookseller, saw in the play an influence even more demoralizing than that of the Deists,[7] and Sir John Hawkins, who disliked Swift, his works, his politics, and his friends, denounced the play in terms so strong as to defeat his purpose.[8] Sir Walter Scott, discussing the moral effect of *Tom Jones*, supports Johnson's vindication of *The Beggar's Opera*.[9] Colley Cibber

[1] Boswell's *Life of Johnson*, II, 367-8 ; Johnson's *Lives of the Poets*, II, 278.
[2] Boswell's *Life of Johnson*, II, 367-8.
[3] *Johnsoniana*, London, 1836, p. 502. See also Nichols's *Literary Anecdotes of the Eighteenth Century*, II, 400, and Boswell's *Life of Johnson*, II, 367, note 1.
[4] Boswell's *Life of Johnson*, II, 367, note 1.
[5] *Some Account of the English Stage*, III, 223-4 ; *Annual Register* for 1773, 2nd ed., London, 1776, p. 132.
[6] *Letters of Horace Walpole*, VIII, 354.
[7] Nichols's *Literary Anecdotes*, I, 703.
[8] Hawkins's *History of Music*, V, 317.
[9] Scott's *Miscellaneous Works*, III, 107.

who, having refused the play as already stated, must have regarded it with feelings even more complicated than those of the fox when looking at the proverbial grapes, makes an original suggestion as to Gay's motive in writing the work.

'I will grant,' he says, 'that in his *Beggar's Opera*, he had more skilfully gratify'd the Public Taste, than all the brightest Authors that ever writ before him; and I have sometimes thought, from the Modesty of his Motto, *Nos haec novimus esse nihil*, that he gave them that Performance, as a Satyr upon the Depravity of their Judgment (as Ben Jonson, of old, was said to have given his *Bartholomew-Fair*, in Ridicule of the vulgar Taste, which had dislik'd his *Sejanus*) and that, by artfully seducing them, to be the Champions of the Immoralities he himself detested, he should be amply reveng'd on their former Severity, and Ignorance.'[1]

But despite fears in some quarters for the cause of public virtue, *The Beggar's Opera* was deemed sufficiently innocuous to be acted by children on 1 January 1729, a performance which was repeated on the following eight days; the Prince of Wales commanding it on one or more of these occasions.[2] And at least once the play has been used to point a moral, as well as to adorn a tale, for Chetwood, historian of English drama, informs us:

I do not pretend to set up for a Monitor; but every Stage Performer would find his Account in reforming the Stage, as well as themselves. I do not mean this Admonition to any particular Theatre, but all in general, at Home and Abroad; for our Plantations in *America* have been voluntarily visited by some Itinerants; *Jamaica*, in particular. I had an Account, from a Gentleman who was possess'd of a large Estate in the Island, that a Company, in the Year 1733 came there, and clear'd a large Sum of Money; where they might have made moderate Fortunes, if they had not been too busy with the Growth of the Country. They receiv'd 370 Pistoles the first Night, to the *Beggar's Opera*; but within the Space of two Months they bury'd their third *Polly*, and two of their Men. The gentlemen of the Island, for some Time, took their turns upon the Stage, to keep up the Diversion; but this did not hold long; for, in two Months more, there were but one old Man, a Boy, and a Woman of the Company, left. The rest died,

---

[1] *Apology*, pp. 141-2.
[2] *Some Account of the English Stage*, III, 238; *Notes and Queries*, 1st Series, I, 178.

either with the Country-Distemper, or the common Beverage of the Place, the noble Spirit of Rum-punch, which is generally fatal to New-comers. The shatter'd Remains, with upwards of 2,000 Pistoles in Bank, embark'd for *Carolina*, to join another Company at *Charlestown*, but were cast away on the Voyage. Had the Company been more blest with the Virtue of Sobriety, &c. they might, perhaps, have liv'd to carry home the Liberality of those generous Islanders.[1]

> ' Duplex libelli dos est : quod risum movet,
> Et quod prudenti vitam consilio monet ! ' [2]

II. *The Beggar's Opera* was, however, influenced by forces other than the political ambitions and circumstances of Gay's life at the time. In form it was shaped by the battle then raging in England between the exotic Italian opera and the native drama.

Despite the merits of Purcell's *Dido and Aeneas*, the close of the Seventeenth Century found English opera in decay, and the opening of the Eighteenth provided an excellent oppor-tunity for the introduction into England of Italian opera, which had overrun France. From France it rapidly spread to England. At first it did not appear in a completely foreign form with Italian words and singers.[3] In 1705 Clayton's *Arsinoe*—a version of an opera produced at Bologna in 1677— was acted by English singers in the English language, but 'after the Italian manner.'[4] But when Handel arrived in England in 1710 he found Italian opera installed, for in that year *Alma-hide* was sung throughout in Italian, the first of many such that were to follow.[5]

' The Italian manner ' consisted in the adherence to certain arbitrary rules of operatic treatment, the effect of which was to ruin the dramatic possibilities of the plot in opera. For ex-ample, there must be six principal characters, three men and three women. The first woman must be a high soprano. The first man, who must take the part of the hero of the piece, must be an artificial soprano. The second man and woman might be either sopranos or contraltos. At least one air in each act

---

[1] *A General History of the Stage*, by W. R. Chetwood, London, 1749.
[2] Phaedrus, *Fables*, Bk. I, Prologue, 3 : 'The book has a double portion : it moves to laughter, and by its counsel teaches a wise man how to live.'
[3] *The Age of Bach and Handel*, p. 191 *et seq.*
[4] *Ibid.*, p. 206. [5] *Ibid.*, p. 207.

must be given to each of the principal singers, and the airs themselves were divided into five classes, no two airs in the same class being allowed to follow one another immediately. There must also be a duet for the first man and woman, and at the end the principal singers only must unite in a *coro*, as it was called.[1]

Amidst such arbitrary conventions, dramatic fitness disintegrated, and it is not strange that literary critics at any rate soon united in condemning the public taste which had abandoned the regular drama for its foreign rival. Addison attacked the fashionable amusement in his writings,[2] besides attempting a counterblast in his English opera *Rosamond*, which appeared in 1707, but was a complete failure. A similar attempt by John Hughes[3] also failed, and the 'exotick and irrational entertainment,' as Johnson called it,[4] swept down all opposition.

In the year 1726 an additional interest to the devotees of Italian opera appeared in the rivalry between Francesca Cuzzoni and Faustina Bordini, the two leading Italian singers in England at the time. They had indeed been rivals from the first day they set foot on the stage, appearing in Gasparini's *Lamano*, at Venice, in 1719. In England their rivalry reached its zenith. Each had numerous supporters, and the audience took sides, each side hissing the heroine of the other. It became the fashion to pit each singer against her rival, while Handel in *Alessandro* wrote for them a duet in which the two voices crossed.[5] So bitter was the personal feeling between the two ladies, that once when both were guests in the home of Lady Walpole, mother of Horace Walpole, she succeeded in enticing each to sing, only by luring the other out of the room on the pretext of examining some china.[6] When the last performance of Buoncini's *Astyanax* was given (6 June 1727) in which Cuzzoni sang Andromache to Faustina's Hermione, the struggle came to a climax.

[1] *Age of Bach and Handel*, pp. 204-5.
[2] For a list of these see Johnson's *Lives of the Poets*, II, 165-6.
[3] Hawkins denies Johnson's belief that Hughes opposed it. Johnson's *Works*, ed. Hawkins, 1787, III, 114.
[4] Johnson's *Lives of the Poets*, II, 160.
[5] *Age of Bach and Handel*, pp. 210-11.
[6] *Ibid.*, p. 211.

The contention at first was only carried on by hissing on one side, and clapping on the other; but proceeded, at length, to the melodious use of cat-calls, and other accompaniments, which manifested the zeal and politeness of that illustrious assembly.[1]

That night marked the decline of Italian opera in England and the failure of the Royal Academy of Music which, founded in 1720, had strongly supported Handel and the Italian opera.

When in 1728 *The Beggar's Opera* appeared, its immediate and overwhelming popularity gave the *coup de grâce* to the moribund Italian opera. Seeing that the foreign opera had already passed its zenith, Pope and Swift may mislead when they state that Gay's play overthrew it, an assertion which Sir John Hawkins, historian of music and biographer of Johnson, denied.[2] Nevertheless, appearing as it did when the fortunes of Italian opera were in a critical position, and accelerating and completing a process of decay already begun, *The Beggar's Opera* was popularly supposed to have killed the hitherto fashionable entertainment.

Gay, writing to inform Swift of the success of his play, adds:

Lord Cobham says that I should have printed it in Italian over against the English, that the ladies might have understood what they read. The outlandish, as they now call it, opera has been so thin of late that some have called that the *Beggar's Opera*, and if the run continues, I fear I shall have remonstrances drawn up against me by the Royal Academy of Music.[3]

And on 20 March following Gay remarks in another letter to Swift:

There is discourse about the town, that the directors of the Royal Academy of Music design to solicit against its being played on the outlandish opera days, as it is now called.[4]

But whatever Gay's motive in choosing the particular form of his play, whatever its effect upon the cult of Italian opera in England, in writing *The Beggar's Opera*, Gay achieved something greater than the destruction of a rival form of art; he invented a new one. As Johnson says:

[1] *London Journal*, 10 June 1727.
[2] Johnson's *Works*, ed. Hawkins, 1787, III, 209, *n*.
[3] Swift's *Correspondence*, IV, 10-11 (15 February 1728).
[4] *Ibid.*, IV, 16

We owe to Gay the Ballad Opera; a mode of comedy which at first was supposed to delight only by its novelty, but has now by the experience of half a century been found so well accommodated to the disposition of a popular audience that it is likely to keep long possession of the stage. Whether this new drama was the product of judgement or of luck the praise of it must be given to the inventor; and there are many writers read with more reverence to whom such merit of originality cannot be attributed.[1]

Thus Johnson. But to Joseph Warton there came, one might almost imagine, some premonition of the dreary fate that was to befall the pleasure seeker in the theatre of to-day; for in his *Essay on Pope* he refers to Gay's masterpiece in the following sentence:

It was the parent of that most monstrous of all dramatic absurdities, the Comic Opera.[2]

And Genest, recorder of English drama, sorrowfully remarks of *The Beggar's Opera*:

Notwithstanding all the merits of this piece, it is much to be wished that it had never been written, as its success has entailed on us from that time to this, those bastard Comedies styled Operas—most of which have been miserably inferior to the Prototype, and many of them little more than mere vehicles for the Songs.[3]

It is a just charge; but to Warton and Genest it was not granted to see the operas of Gilbert and Sullivan, offspring of which the parent might well be proud.

III. Last, though lack of space prevents more than a mere glance at the matter, there is the relation of Gay's play to the general spirit of his time.

The reasons for the popularity of *The Beggar's Opera* were frequently discussed in the Eighteenth Century. Swift thought that in its humour lay the secret of its appeal to the age.[4]

Boswell records the following conversation which took place at the house of Sir Joshua Reynolds on 25 April 1778:

[1] Johnson's *Lives of the Poets*, II, 282-3.
[2] *Essay on Pope*, II, 315, ed. 1782.
[3] *Some Account of the English Stage*, III, 224.
[4] *Works*, 1824, IX, 92.

Sir Joshua Reynolds. '*The Beggar's Opera* affords a proof how strangely people will differ in opinion about a literary performance. Burke thinks it has no merit.' Johnson. 'It was refused by one of the houses ; but I should have thought it would succeed, not from any great excellence in the writing, but from the novelty, and the general spirit and gaiety of the piece, which keeps the audience always attentive, and dismisses them in good humour.'[1]

But the disputants were too near to the event to see clearly. The fact is, surely, that in its own way, and on a somewhat low and popular level, the play, apart from the appeal of its music, songs, and setting, is as truly representative of the age which produced it as is Pope's *Rape of the Lock* in another manner, and on a different level.

The 'Augustan Age' was an age of 'Reason.' It was immensely proud of the fact, and could not forget it. From the opening of the century until the death of Swift in 1745 (to take a convenient date) the age manifested an almost pathetically innocent faith in the power of reason to solve the problems incidental to human life and human happiness. As one anonymous poet sang in 1726:

> Still shall each kind returning season
> Sufficient for our wishes give;
> For we will live a life of reason,
> And that's the only life to live![2]

The principle was no doubt excellent, but, unfortunately, the reason men decided to worship was a narrow, practical reason, blind to all aspects of life that could not be stated with logical clearness and precision. Inspired by the influence of the empirical philosophy of Hobbes and Locke, and its continuation by Hume, they closed their eyes to whatever was not 'reasonable' in human nature and in life, and determined that for themselves it should no longer exist. The 'passions,' they said, were man's chief enemy, and therefore the passions must be stamped out. Hence arose an ideal of stoicism, of happiness by way of negation, of a self-completeness which

[1] Boswell's *Life of Johnson*, III, 321.
[2] Lewis's Miscellany, 1726. *Song from the Ancient British.*

should make one independent of others, by the suppression of emotion. The thought dominates the literature of the age from *Gulliver's Travels* to *Rasselas*; but while the former seeks to show that the ideal of ' reason ' has not been attained, the latter also bears witness to its passing. Of many examples which might be given, we choose Pomfret's poem, which appeared in 1700, as expressing the aim of the dawning century.

REASON

The passions still predominant will rule,
Ungovern'd, rude, not bred in Reason's school;
Our understanding they with darkness fill,
Cause strong corruptions, and pervert the will;
On these the soul, as on some flowing tide,
Must sit, and on the raging billows ride,
Hurried away; for how can be withstood
The impetuous torrent of the boiling blood?
Begone, false hopes, for all our learning's vain;
Can we be free, where these the rule maintain?
These are the tools of knowledge which we use;
The spirits, heated, will strange things produce;
Tell me, whoe'er the passions could control,
Or from the body disengage the soul;
Till this is done, our best pursuits are vain
To conquer truth, and unmix'd knowledge gain.

We find this same desire for freedom from emotion in Mrs. Greville's *Prayer for Indifference*, as late as 1762, but in Cowper's *Reply* to that *Prayer* we see the protest of the spirit of revolt, which marks the dawn of the new age of Romance.

But it was in the early years of the century, before this conception had been tested by life itself, that it exerted its greatest influence. For a time Pope and Swift believed in it, but their insight was too keen, and the lessons life brought them were too bitter for them to remain deluded to the end; and their letters show that the close of their lives was darkened by the realization of a disproved faith.

Gay, however, ever ready to follow where his friends led, and dying long before them, kept up the popular pose until his death. He will be a stoic of a kind, and writes his own epitaph in that spirit:

> Life is a jest, and all things show it.
> I thought so once, and now I know it.

They might be the words of Macheath upon the scaffold. And the reason is obvious. Macheath is Gay's ideal in the flesh. If Macheath had hoped for court favour and been disappointed, he would have written as Gay did:

As I am used to disappointments I can bear them: but as I can have no more hopes, I can no more be disappointed, so that I am in a blessed condition.

And then he would have danced daintily, trolling forth a tol de rol of careless disdain. And so, in presenting his ideal *poseur*, Gay presented a popular and debased image of the conception which had largely influenced the spirit of the time. Untouched by true emotion, without affection for others, complete in himself, cynical and gay, Macheath will take all of pleasure that life can give, as he trips his dainty way along the primrose path, singing:

> I sipt each Flower,
> I chang'd ev'ry Hour.

Nor will death have any terrors for this gay stoic: He will meet it dainty and debonair, living and dying like an aristocrat of the French Revolution. He is the man of reason, of intellect without emotion, the spirit of the age reflected in a distorting mirror; and so, when arrested, and with the shadow of the gallows upon him, he airily sings:

> At the Tree I shall suffer with Pleasure,
> At the Tree I shall suffer with Pleasure,

for, with a glance at the women about him,

> Let me go where I will,
> In all kinds of ill,
> I shall find no such Furies as these are.

Yes, Gay's epitaph is certainly Macheath's.

the play was written, and the most important is Pope's remark in (*c*), that Gay wrote it in the same house with Pope and Swift, for, in that case, it must have been written during one of Swift's two visits to Twicken-ham in 1726 and 1727.

In my introduction to *Polly*, I followed the statement in Sir Henry Craik's *Life of Swift* (2nd ed., 1894, II, 137) that Gay was busy writing the play during Swift's first visit, in 1726. But no authority is cited for the remark. Upon examination, I incline to place the commencement of *The Beggar's Opera* during the visit of 1727, for the following reasons:

(1) There is no allusion to the play in the correspondence of Pope, Swift, and Gay, between Swift's departure from England in 1726 and his return on 9 April 1727. While after Swift's departure in 1727 the play is constantly referred to, from the moment of completion, throughout the period of its presentation on the stage.

(2) Gay was, we know, busy in 1726 writing his *Fables*, which appeared in the spring of 1727. Throughout the period in which they were being written, they are constantly referred to in the correspond-ence of the friends. Scott, in his *Life of Swift*, apparently dates the play in 1727. See *The Prose Works of Sir Walter Scott*, 6 vols., Edin-burgh, 1834, vol. ii.

On these grounds, both positive and negative, and so com-plementary, I believe my attempt at an imaginative reconstruction of the progress of *The Beggar's Opera* is at least in accordance with probability. Mr. Lewis Melville, while not stating definitely the year in which *The Beggar's Opera* was begun, apparently believes, like myself, that it was in 1727, not 1726, for he remarks:

Dilatory as Gay always was, he contrived to finish his opera by about the end of the year (*Life and Letters of John Gay*, p. 79).

It is hardly necessary to point out, that although Gay probably began the work before the death of George I, he had ample time in which to revise it and sharpen its sting, between the overthrow of his hopes of court favour in October 1727 and its first appearance on the stage on 29 January 1728.

NOTE II

I⊤ seems highly probable that Swift attempted to see *The Beggar's Opera* when it was being acted in Dublin ; that because of his ecclesiastical calling and of the political nature of the play he went to the theatre in mufti, that he was recognized, and that unpleasant comments were made which caused him to withdraw without seeing it. The grounds for this supposition are as follow:

(1) Swift's remark in a letter to Pope, which reveals the fact that so late as 10 May 1728 Swift, despite his great interest in the play, had not seen it acted.

'Mr. Gay's opera,' he writes, 'has been acted here twenty times, and my Lord Lieutenant tells me it is very well performed ; he has seen it often, and approves it much (Swift's *Correspondence*, IV, 29).

(2) The following passage in Swift's defence of the play in *The Intelligencer* :

I am assured that several worthy clergymen in this city (Dublin) went privately to see *The Beggar's Opera* represented : and that the fleering coxcombs in the pit amused themselves with making discoveries, and spreading the names of those gentlemen round the audience. I shall not pretend to vindicate a clergyman who would appear openly in his habit at the theatre, with such a vicious crew as might probably stand round him, at such comedies and profane tragedies as are often represented. Besides I know very well, that persons of their function are bound to avoid the appearance of evil or of giving cause of offence. But when the lords chancellors who are keepers of the king's conscience ; when the judges of the land, whose title is reverend ; when ladies who are bound by the rules of their sex to the strictest decency, appear in the theatre without censure ; I cannot understand why a young clergyman, who comes concealed out of curiosity to see an innocent and moral play, should be so highly condemned ; nor do I much approve the rigour of a great prelate who said, 'he hoped none of his clergy were there.' I am glad to hear there are no weightier objections against that reverend body, planted in this city, and I wish there never may (Swift's *Works*, 1824, IX).

Is there not a warmth as of personal indignation on behalf of the ' young clergyman who comes concealed ' ? Is it possible that interested as he was in the play of an intimate friend, a play which he had originated, and holding such views as to the attendance of clergy at the theatre, Swift should have made no attempt to see *The Beggar's Opera* himself ? The change from ' several worthy clergymen ' to ' a young clergyman ' later may have some significance in this way.

SOME OF THE WORKS CONSULTED

Where not otherwise stated, the place of publication is London

An Apology for the Life of Mr. Colley Cibber, Written by Himself. 1740.
Annual Register for the Year 1773. 1776.
Correspondence of Jonathan Swift, ed. F. E. Ball. 6 vols. 1910-1914.
Gay's Chair with a Sketch of his Life, by J. Baller, ed. Henry Lee.
    1820.
Johnsoniana. 1836.
Letters from Dr. Thomas Herring to William Duncombe. 1777.
Letters from Horace Walpole, ed. Mrs. Paget Toynbee. 16 vols.
    Oxford, 1903.
Letters of Philip Dormer Stanhope, Earl of Chesterfield, ed. Lord Mahon.
    5 vols. 1845-1853.
Letters to and from Henrietta, Countess of Suffolk, ed. J. W. Croker.
    2 vols. 1824.
Lives of the English Poets, by Samuel Johnson, ed. G. B. Hill. 3 vols.
    Oxford, 1905.
Poems of John Gay, ed. John Underhill. 2 vols. n.d.
Prose Works of Sir Walter Scott. 6 vols. Edinburgh, 1834.
Works of Alexander Pope, ed. J. Warton and others. 9 vols. 1797.
Works of Alexander Pope, ed. W. Elwin and J. Courthope. 10 vols.
    1871-1889.
Works of Jonathan Swift, ed. Sir Walter Scott. Edinburgh, 1824.

Baker, D. E. : *Biographia Dramatica.* 2 vols. 1782.
Boswell, James : *The Life of Samuel Johnson*, ed. G. B. Hill. 6 vols.
    Oxford, 1887.
Chetwood, W. R. : *A General History of the Stage.* 1749.
Coxe, William : *Memoirs of the Life and Administration of Sir Robert
    Walpole.* 3 vols. 1798.
Craik, Sir Henry : *The Life of Jonathan Swift.* 2 vols. 1894.
Edwards, Sutherland : *History of the Opera.* 2 vols. 1862.
Genest, John : *Some Account of the English Stage from the Restoration in
    1660 to 1830.* 10 vols. Bath, 1832.
Hawkins, Sir John : *A General History of the Science and Practice of
    Music.* 5 vols. 1776.

Herring, Thomas : *Seven Sermons on Public Occasions.*   1763.

Hervey, Lord John : *Memoirs of the Reign of George the Second,* ed. J. W. Croker.   3 vols.   1884.

Kidson, Frank : *The Beggar's Opera.*   Cambridge, 1922.

Maitland, J. A. Fuller : *The Age of Bach and Handel.*   Oxford, 1902.

Melville, Lewis : *Life and Letters of John Gay.*   London, 1921.

Nichols, John : *Literary Anecdotes of the Eighteenth Century.*   6 vols. 1812.

Pearce, Charles E. : *Polly Peachum.*   1913.

Spence, Joseph : *Anecdotes, Observations, and Characters of Books and Men,* ed. S. W. Singer.   1858.

Warton, Joseph : *Essay on the Genius and Writings of Pope.*   2 vols. Vol. I, 1762 ; Vol. II, 1782.

Wright, Thomas : *Caricature History of the Georges.*   1904.

THE BEGGAR'S OPERA

JOHN GAY.

From the Original Picture, painted by W. Hogarth.
Executed in Lithography by M. Gauci.

London, Published by the Proprietor, June 1826 at the Gothic Hall Pall Mall.
Printed by C. Hullmandel.

J. Netherclift, fecit.

THE
BEGGAR's
OPERA.

As it is Acted at the

THEATRE-ROYAL

IN

LINCOLNS-INN FIELDS.

Written by Mr. *G A Y.*

————— *Nos hæc noviſſimus eſſe nihil.*　　Mart.

The **THIRD EDITION:**
With the **OUVERTURE** in **SCORE,**
The **S O N G S,** *and the* **B A S S E S,**

(The OUVERTURE and BASSES Compos'd by Dr. *PEPUSCH*)
Curiouſly Engrav'd on COPPER PLATES.

L O N D O N:
Printed for J o h n W a t t s, at the Printing-Office in *Wild-Court*, near *Lincoln's-Inn Fields.*
M DCC XXIX.

A
TABLE of the SONGS.

ACT I.

III

ACT III.

A TABLE OF SONGS

Dramatis Personae

MEN

Mr. Peachum.
Lockit.
Macheath.
Filch.
Jemmy Twitcher,
Crook-finger'd Jack,
Wat Dreary,
Robin *of* Bagshot, } Macheath's
Nimming Ned, *Gang.*
Harry Padington,
Mat *of the* Mint,
Ben Budge,
Beggar.
Player.
    Constables, Drawers, Turnkey, &c.

WOMEN

Mrs. Peachum.
Polly Peachum.
Lucy Lockit.
Diana Trapes.
Mrs. Coaxer,
Dolly Trull,
Mrs. Vixen,
Betty Doxy, } *Women of the*
Jenny Diver, *Town.*
Mrs. Slammekin,
Suky Tawdry,
Molly Brazen,

INTRODUCTION

BEGGAR, PLAYER

Beggar.

IF Poverty be a Title to Poetry, I am sure nobody can dispute mine. I own myself of the Company of Beggars; and I make one at their Weekly Festivals at St. *Giles's*. I have a small Yearly Salary for my Catches, and am welcome to a Dinner there whenever I please, which is more than most Poets can say.

Player. As we live by the Muses, it is but Gratitude in us to encourage Poetical Merit wherever we find it. The Muses, contrary to all other Ladies, pay no Distinction to Dress, and never partially mistake the Pertness of Embroidery for Wit, nor the Modesty of Want for Dulness. Be the Author who he will, we push his Play as far as it will go. So (though you are in Want) I wish you success heartily.

Beggar. This piece I own was originally writ for the celebrating the Marriage of *James Chanter* and *Moll Lay,* two most excellent Ballad-Singers. I have introduced the Similes that are in all your celebrated *Operas ;* The *Swallow,* the *Moth,* the *Bee,* the *Ship,* the *Flower,* &c. Besides, I have a Prison-Scene, which the Ladies always reckon charmingly pathetick. As to the Parts, I have observed such a nice Impartiality to our two Ladies that it is impossible for either of them to take Offence. I hope I may be forgiven, that I have not made my Opera throughout unnatural, like those in vogue ; for I have no Recitative ; excepting this, as I have consented to have neither Prologue nor Epilogue, it must be allowed an Opera in all its Forms. The Piece indeed hath been heretofore frequently represented by ourselves in our Great Room at St. *Giles's,* so that I cannot too often acknowledge your Charity in bringing it now on the Stage.

Player. But I see it is time for us to withdraw ; the Actors are preparing to begin. Play away the Overture.   [*Exeunt.*

THE
BEGGAR'S OPERA

ACT I. SCENE I.

SCENE, Peachum's *House*.

Peachum *sitting at a Table with a large Book of Accounts before him.*

AIR I.—An old Woman clothed in Gray, &c.

HROUGH all the Employments of Life
  Each Neighbour abuses his Brother;
Whore and Rogue they call Husband and Wife:
  All Professions be-rogue one another:
The Priest calls the Lawyer a Cheat,
 The Lawyer be-knaves the Divine:
And the Statesman, because he's so great,
 Thinks his Trade as honest as mine.

A Lawyer is an honest Employment, so is mine. Like me too he acts in a double Capacity, both against Rogues and for 'em; for 'tis but fitting that we should protect and encourage Cheats, since we live by them.

SCENE II.

PEACHUM, FILCH.

Filch. Sir, Black *Moll* hath sent word her Trial comes on in the Afternoon, and she hopes you will order Matters so as to bring her off.

Peachum. Why, she may plead her Belly at worst; to my Knowledge she hath taken care of that Security. But, as the Wench is very active and industrious, you may satisfy her that I'll soften the Evidence.

Filch. *Tom Gagg*, Sir, is found guilty.

Peachum. A lazy Dog! When I took him the time before, I told him what he would come to if he did not mend his Hand. This is Death without Reprieve. I may venture to Book him. [*writes.*] For *Tom Gagg*, forty Pounds. Let *Betty Sly* know that I'll save her from Transportation, for I can get more by her staying in *England*.

Filch. Betty hath brought more Goods into our Lock to-year than any five of the Gang; and in truth, 'tis a pity to lose so good a Customer.

Peachum. If none of the Gang take her off, she

may, in the common course of Business, live a
Twelve-month longer.   I love to let Women scape.
A good Sportsman always lets the Hen Partridges
fly, because the Breed of the Game depends upon
them. Besides, here the Law allows us no Reward;
there is nothing to be got by the Death of Women
———except our Wives.

Filch. Without dispute, she is a fine Woman !
'Twas to her I was obliged for my Education, and
(to say a bold Word) she hath trained up more young
Fellows to the Business than the Gaming table.

Peachum. Truly, Filch, thy Observation is right.
We and the Surgeons are more beholden to Women
than all the Professions besides.

AIR II.——The bonny gray-ey'd Morn, &c.

Filch.

'Tis Woman that seduces all Mankind,
   By her we first were taught the wheedling Arts:
Her very Eyes can cheat : when most she's kind,
   She tricks us of our Money with our Hearts.
For her, like Wolves by Night we roam for Prey,
   And practise ev'ry Fraud to bribe her Charms;
For Suits of Love, like Law, are won by Pay,
   And Beauty must be fee'd into our Arms.

Peachum. But make haste to *Newgate*, Boy, and
let my Friends know what I intend; for I love to
make them easy one way or other.

Filch. When a Gentleman is long kept in suspence, Penitence may break his Spirit ever after. Besides, Certainty gives a Man a good Air upon his Trial, and makes him risque another without Fear or Scruple. But I'll away, for 'tis a Pleasure to be the Messenger of Comfort to Friends in Affliction.

SCENE III.

PEACHUM.

But 'tis now high time to look about me for a decent Execution against next Sessions. I hate a lazy Rogue, by whom one can get nothing 'till he is hang'd. A Register of the Gang, [*Reading*] Crook-finger'd *Jack*. A Year and a half in the Service; Let me see how much the Stock owes to his Industry; one, two, three, four, five Gold Watches, and seven Silver ones. A mighty clean-handed Fellow! Sixteen Snuff-boxes, five of them of true Gold. Six Dozen of Handkerchiefs, four silver-hilted Swords, half a Dozen of Shirts, three Tye-Periwigs, and a Piece of Broad-Cloth. Considering these are only the Fruits of his leisure Hours, I don't know a prettier Fellow, for no Man alive hath a more engaging Presence of Mind upon the Road. *Wat Dreary*, alias *Brown Will*, an irregular Dog, who hath an underhand way of disposing of his Goods. I'll try him only for a Sessions or two longer upon his Good-behaviour. *Harry Padington*, a poor petty-larceny Rascal, without the least Genius; that

Fellow, though he were to live these six Months, will never come to the Gallows with any Credit. Slippery *Sam*; he goes off the next Sessions, for the Villain hath the Impudence to have views of following his Trade as a Tailor, which he calls an honest Employment. *Mat* of the *Mint*; listed not above a Month ago, a promising sturdy Fellow, and diligent in his way; somewhat too bold and hasty, and may raise good Contributions on the Public, if he does not cut himself short by Murder. *Tom Tipple*, a guzzling soaking Sot, who is always too drunk to stand himself, or to make others stand. A Cart is absolutely necessary for him. *Robin* of *Bagshot*, alias *Gorgon*, alias *Bluff Bob*, alias *Carbuncle*, alias *Bob Booty*.

SCENE IV.

PEACHUM, Mrs. PEACHUM.

Mrs. Peachum. What of *Bob Booty*, Husband? I hope nothing bad hath betided him. You know, my Dear, he's a favourite Customer of mine. 'Twas he made me a present of this Ring.

Peachum. I have set his Name down in the Black List, that's all, my Dear; he spends his Life among Women, and as soon as his Money is gone, one or other of the Ladies will hang him for the Reward, and there's forty Pounds lost to us forever.

Mrs. Peachum. You know, my Dear, I never meddle in matters of Death; I always leave those Affairs to you. Women indeed are bitter bad Judges in these cases, for they are so partial to the Brave that they think every Man handsome who is going to the Camp or the Gallows.

AIR III.—Cold and raw, &c.

If any Wench Venus's *Girdle wear,*
  Though she be never so ugly;
Lilies and Roses will quickly appear,
  And her Face look wond'rous smugly.
Beneath the left Ear so fit but a Cord,
  (A Rope so charming a Zone is!)
The Youth in his Cart hath the Air of a Lord,
  And we cry, There dies an Adonis!

But really, Husband, you should not be too hard-hearted, for you never had a finer, braver set of Men than at present. We have not had a Murder among them all, these seven Months. And truly, my Dear, that is a great Blessing.

Peachum. What a dickens is the Woman always a whimpring about Murder for? No Gentleman is ever look'd upon the worse for killing a Man in his own Defence; and if Business cannot be carried on without it, what would you have a Gentleman do?

Mrs. Peachum. If I am in the wrong, my Dear, you must excuse me, for no body can help the Frailty of an over-scrupulous Conscience.

Peachum. Murder is as fashionable a Crime as a

MISS FENTON AS POLLY PEACHUM

J. Elly; Pinx.   J. Faber Fecit 1728.

MR. WALKER AS CAPTAIN MACHEATH

Man can be guilty of. How many fine Gentlemen
have we in *Newgate* every Year, purely upon that
Article! If they have wherewithal to persuade the
Jury to bring it in Manslaughter, what are they the
worse for it? So, my Dear, have done upon this
Subject. Was Captain *Macheath* here this Morning,
for the Bank-Notes he left with you last Week?

Mrs. Peachum. Yes, my Dear; and though the
Bank hath stopt Payment, he was so cheerful and
so agreeable! Sure there is not a finer Gentleman
upon the Road than the Captain! If he comes
from *Bagshot* at any reasonable Hour, he hath
promis'd to make one this Evening with *Polly* and
me, and *Bob Booty* at a Party of Quadrille. Pray,
my Dear, is the Captain rich?

Peachum. The Captain keeps too good Company
ever to grow rich. Marybone and the Chocolate-
houses are his Undoing. The Man that proposes
to get Money by Play should have the Education
of a fine Gentleman, and be train'd up to it from
his Youth.

Mrs. Peachum. Really, I am sorry upon *Polly's*
Account the Captain hath not more Discretion.
What Business hath he to keep Company with
Lords and Gentlemen? he should leave them to
prey upon one another.

Peachum. Upon *Polly's* Account! What a Plague
does the Woman mean?——Upon *Polly's* Account!

Mrs. Peachum. Captain *Macheath* is very fond
of the Girl.

Peachum. And what then?

Mrs. Peachum. If I have any Skill in the Ways of Women, I am sure *Polly* thinks him a very pretty Man.

Peachum. And what then? You would not be so mad to have the Wench marry him! Gamesters and Highwaymen are generally very good to their Whores, but they are very Devils to their Wives.

Mrs. Peachum. But if *Polly* should be in Love, how should we help her, or how can she help herself? Poor Girl, I am in the utmost Concern about her.

AIR IV.—Why is your faithful Slave disdain'd? &c.

If Love the Virgin's Heart invade,
How, like a Moth, the simple Maid
   Still plays about the Flame!
If soon she be not made a Wife,
Her Honour's sing'd, and then for Life.
   She's—what I dare not name.

Peachum. Look ye, Wife. A handsome Wench in our way of Business is as profitable as at the Bar of a *Temple* Coffee-House, who looks upon it as her livelihood to grant every Liberty but one. You see I would indulge the Girl as far as prudently we can. In anything, but Marriage! After that, my Dear, how shall we be safe? Are we not then in her Husband's Power? For a Husband hath the absolute Power over all a Wife's Secrets but her own. If the Girl had the Discretion of a Court-Lady, who can have a Dozen young Fellows at her Ear without complying with one, I should not matter it; but *Polly* is Tinder, and a Spark will at once set her on a Flame. Married! If the Wench does not know her own Profit, sure she knows her own Pleasure better than to make herself a Property! My Daughter to me should be, like a Court-Lady to a Minister of State, a Key to the whole Gang. Married! If the Affair is not already done, I'll terrify her from it, by the Example of our Neighbours.

Mrs. Peachum. May-hap, my Dear, you may injure the Girl. She loves to imitate the fine Ladies, and she may only allow the Captain Liberties in the view of Interest.

Peachum. But 'tis your Duty, my Dear, to warn the Girl against her Ruin, and to instruct her how to make the most of her Beauty. I'll go to her this moment, and sift her. In the mean time, Wife, rip out the Coronets and Marks of these Dozen of Cambric Handkerchiefs, for I can dispose of them this Afternoon to a Chap in the City.

SCENE V.

Mrs. PEACHUM.

Never was a Man more out of the way in an Argument than my Husband! Why must our *Polly*, forsooth, differ from her Sex, and love only her Husband? And why must *Polly's* Marriage, contrary to all Observation, make her the less followed by other Men? All Men are Thieves in Love, and like a Woman the better for being another's Property.

AIR V.—Of all the simple Things we do, &c.

A Maid is like the Golden Ore,
*   Which hath Guineas intrinsical in't,*
Whose Worth is never known, before
*   It is try'd and imprest in the Mint.*
A Wife's like a Guinea in Gold,
*   Stampt with the Name of her Spouse;*
Now here, now there; is bought, or is sold;
*   And is current in every House.*

SCENE VI.

Mrs. PEACHUM, FILCH.

Mrs. Peachum. Come hither, *Filch.* I am as fond of this Child, as though my Mind misgave me he were my own. He hath as fine a Hand at picking a Pocket as a Woman, and is as nimble-finger'd as a Juggler. If an unlucky Session does not cut the Rope of thy Life, I pronounce, Boy, thou wilt be a great Man in History. Where was your Post last Night, my Boy?

Filch. I ply'd at the Opera, Madam; and considering 'twas neither dark nor rainy, so that there was no great Hurry in getting Chairs and Coaches, made a tolerable Hand on't. These seven Handkerchiefs, Madam.

Mrs. Peachum. Colour'd ones, I see. They are of sure Sale from our Warehouse at *Redriff* among the Seamen.

Filch. And this Snuff-box.

Mrs. Peachum. Set in Gold! A pretty Encouragement this to a young Beginner.

Filch. I had a fair Tug at a charming Gold Watch. Pox take the Tailors for making the Fobs so deep and narrow! It stuck by the way, and I was forc'd to make my Escape under a Coach. Really, Madam, I fear I shall be cut off in the Flower of my Youth, so that every now and then (since I was pumpt) I have Thoughts of taking up and going to Sea.

Mrs. Peachum. You should go to *Hockley in the Hole*, and to *Marybone*, Child, to learn Valour. These are the Schools that have bred so many brave Men. I thought, Boy, by this time, thou hadst lost Fear as well as Shame. Poor Lad! how little does he know as yet of the *Old Baily*! For the first Fact I'll insure thee from being hang'd; and going to Sea, *Filch*, will come time enough upon a Sentence of Transportation. But now, since you have nothing better to do, ev'n go to your Book, and learn your Catechism; for really a Man makes but an ill Figure in the Ordinary's Paper, who cannot give a satisfactory Answer to his Questions. But, hark you, my Lad. Don't tell me a Lye; for you know I hate a Liar. Do you know of anything that hath pass'd between Captain *Macheath* and our *Polly*?

Filch. I beg you, Madam, don't ask me; for I

must either tell a Lye to you or to Miss *Polly*; for I promis'd her I would not tell.

Mrs. Peachum. But when the Honour of our Family is concern'd——

Filch. I shall lead a sad Life with Miss *Polly*, if ever she comes to know that I told you. Besides, I would not willingly forfeit my own Honour by betraying any body.

Mrs. Peachum. Yonder comes my Husband and *Polly.* Come, *Filch*, you shall go with me into my own Room, and tell me the whole Story. I'll give thee a most delicious Glass of a Cordial that I keep for my own drinking.

SCENE VII.

PEACHUM, POLLY.

Polly. I know as well as any of the fine Ladies how to make the most of myself and of my Man too. A Woman knows how to be mercenary, though she hath never been in a Court or at an Assembly. We have it in our Natures, Papa. If I allow Captain *Macheath* some trifling Liberties, I have this Watch and other visible Marks of his Favour to show for it. A Girl who cannot grant some Things, and refuse what is most material, will make but a poor hand of her Beauty, and soon be thrown upon the Common.

AIR VI.—What shall I do to show how much
I love her, &c.

Virgins are like the fair Flower in its Lustre,
  Which in the Garden enamels the Ground;
Near it the Bees in play flutter and cluster,
  And gaudy Butterflies frolick around.
But, when once pluck'd, 'tis no longer alluring,
  To Covent-Garden 'tis sent (as yet sweet),
There fades, and shrinks, and grows past all enduring
  Rots, stinks, and dies, and is trod under feet.

Peachum. You know, *Polly,* I am not against your
toying and trifling with a Customer in the way of
Business, or to get out a Secret, or so. But if I find
out that you have play'd the Fool and are married,
you Jade you, I'll cut your Throat, Hussy. Now
you know my Mind.

SCENE VIII.

PEACHUM, POLLY, Mrs. PEACHUM.

AIR VII.—Oh *London* is a fine Town.

  Mrs. Peachum, in a very great Passion.
Our Polly *is a sad Slut! nor heeds what we have*
    taught her.
I wonder any Man alive will ever rear a Daughter!
For she must have both Hoods and Gowns, and Hoops
    to swell her Pride,

With Scarfs and Stays, and Gloves and Lace; and
she will have Men beside;
And when she's drest with Care and Cost, all tempt-
ing, fine and gay,
As Men should serve a Cowcumber, she flings herself
away.

Our Polly *is a sad Slut!* &c.

You Baggage! you Hussy! you inconsiderate Jade!
had you been hang'd, it would not have vex'd me,
for that might have been your Misfortune; but to do
such a mad thing by Choice! The Wench is married,
Husband.

Peachum. Married! the Captain is a bold Man,
and will risk anything for Money; to be sure he
believes her a Fortune. Do you think your Mother
and I should have liv'd comfortably so long together,
if ever we had been married? Baggage!

Mrs. Peachum. I knew she was always a proud
Slut; and now the Wench hath play'd the Fool and
Married, because forsooth she would do like the
Gentry. Can you support the Expence of a Husband,
Hussy, in Gaming, Drinking and Whoring? Have
you Money enough to carry on the daily Quarrels of
Man and Wife about who shall squander most? There
are not many Husbands and Wives, who can bear the
Charges of plaguing one another in a handsome way.
If you must be married, could you introduce no body
into our Family but a Highwayman? Why, thou
foolish Jade, thou wilt be as ill-us'd, and as much
neglected, as if thou hadst married a Lord!

MRS. FARREL IN THE PART OF MACHEATH

MR. BANNISTER IN THE CHARACTER
OF POLLY PEACHUM

Peachum. Let not your Anger, my Dear, break through the Rules of Decency, for the Captain looks upon himself in the Military Capacity, as a Gentleman by his Profession. Besides what he hath already, I know he is in a fair way of getting, or of dying; and both these ways, let me tell you, are most excellent Chances for a Wife. Tell me, Hussy, are you ruin'd or no?

Mrs. Peachum. With *Polly's* Fortune, she might very well have gone off to a Person of Distinction. Yes, that you might, you pouting Slut!

Peachum. What is the Wench dumb? Speak, or I'll make you plead by squeezing out an Answer from you. Are you really bound Wife to him, or are you only upon liking?   [*Pinches her.*

Polly. Oh!   [*Screaming.*

Mrs. Peachum. How the Mother is to be pitied who hath handsome Daughters! Locks, Bolts, Bars, and Lectures of Morality are nothing to them: They break through them all. They have as much Pleasure in cheating a Father and Mother, as in cheating at Cards.

Peachum. Why, *Polly*, I shall soon know if you are married, by *Macheath's* keeping from our House.

AIR VIII.—Grim King of the Ghosts, &c.
Polly.
Can Love be control'd by Advice?
    Will Cupid *our Mothers obey?*
Though my Heart were as frozen as Ice,
    At his Flame 'twould have melted away

When he kist me so closely he prest,
  'Twas so sweet that I must have comply'd;
So I thought it both safest and best
  To marry, for fear you should chide.

Mrs. Peachum. Then all the Hopes of our Family are gone for ever and ever!

Peachum. And *Macheath* may hang his Father and Mother-in-law, in hope to get into their Daughter's Fortune.

Polly. I did not marry him (as 'tis the Fashion) coolly and deliberately for Honour or Money. But, I love him.

Mrs. Peachum. Love him! worse and worse! I thought the Girl had been better bred. Oh Husband, Husband! her Folly makes me mad! my Head swims! I'm distracted! I can't support myself——— Oh!   [*Faints.*

Peachum. See, Wench, to what a Condition you have reduc'd your poor Mother! a Glass of Cordial, this instant. How the poor Woman takes it to heart!   [Polly *goes out, and returns with it.* Ah, Hussy, now this is the only Comfort your Mother has left!

Polly. Give her another Glass, Sir! my Mama drinks double the Quantity whenever she is out of Order. This, you see, fetches her.

Mrs. Peachum. The Girl shows such a Readiness, and so much Concern, that I could almost find in my Heart to forgive her.

AIR IX.—O *Jenny*, O *Jenny*, where hast thou been.

O Polly, *you might have toy'd and kist.*
By keeping Men off, you keep them on.

Polly.
But he so teaz'd me,
And he so pleas'd me,
What I did, you must have done.

Mrs. Peachum. Not with a Highwayman.———
You sorry Slut!

Peachum. A Word with you, Wife. 'Tis no new thing for a Wench to take Man without Consent of Parents. You know 'tis the Frailty of Woman, my Dear.

Mrs. Peachum. Yes, indeed, the Sex is frail. But the first time a Woman is frail, she should be somewhat nice methinks, for then or never is the time to make her Fortune. After that, she hath nothing to do but to guard herself from being found out, and she may do what she pleases.

Peachum. Make yourself a little easy; I have a Thought shall soon set all Matters again to rights. Why so melancholy, *Polly*? since what is done cannot be undone, we must all endeavour to make the best of it.

Mrs. Peachum. Well, *Polly*; as far as one Woman can forgive another, I forgive thee.———Your Father is too fond of you, Hussy.

Polly. Then all my Sorrows are at an end.

Mrs. Peachum. A mighty likely Speech in troth, for a Wench who is just married!

AIR X.—*Thomas, I cannot, &c.*

Polly.

I, like a Ship in Storms, was tost;
Yet afraid to put in to Land:
For seiz'd in the Port the Vessel's lost,
Whose Treasure is contreband.
 The Waves are laid,
 My Duty's paid.
O Joy beyond Expression!
 Thus, safe a-shore,
 I ask no more,
My All is in my Possession.

Peachum. I hear Customers in t'other Room: Go, talk with 'em, *Polly*; but come to us again, as soon as they are gone——But, hark ye, Child, if 'tis the Gentleman who was here Yesterday about the Repeating Watch; say, you believe we can't get Intelligence of it till to-morrow. For I lent it to *Suky Straddle*, to make a figure with it to-night at a Tavern in *Drury-Lane*. If t'other Gentleman calls for the Silver-hilted Sword; you know Beetle-brow'd *Jemmy* hath it on, and he doth not come from *Tunbridge* 'till *Tuesday* Night; so that it cannot be had 'till then.

SCENE IX.

PEACHUM, Mrs. PEACHUM.

Peachum. Dear Wife, be a little pacified, Don't let your Passion run away with your Senses. *Polly*, I grant you, hath done a rash thing.

Mrs. Peachum. If she had had only an Intrigue with the Fellow, why the very best Families have excus'd and huddled up a Frailty of that sort. 'Tis Marriage, Husband, that makes it a Blemish.

Peachum. But Money, Wife, is the true Fuller's Earth for Reputations, there is not a Spot or a Stain but what it can take out. A rich Rogue now-a-days is fit Company for any Gentleman; and the World, my Dear, hath not such a Contempt for Roguery as you imagine. I tell you, Wife, I can make this Match turn to our Advantage.

Mrs. Peachum. I am very sensible, Husband, that Captain *Macheath* is worth Money, but I am in doubt whether he hath not two or three Wives already, and then if he should die in a Session or two, *Polly's* Dower would come into Dispute.

Peachum. That, indeed, is a Point which ought to be consider'd.

AIR XI.—A Soldier and a Sailor.

A Fox may steal your Hens, Sir,
A Whore your Health and Pence, Sir,

Your Daughter rob your Chest, Sir,
Your Wife may steal your Rest, Sir.
A Thief your Goods and Plate.
But this is all but picking,
With Rest, Pence, Chest and Chicken;
It ever was decreed, Sir,
If Lawyer's Hand is fee'd, Sir,
He steals your whole Estate.

The Lawyers are bitter Enemies to those in our Way. They don't care that any body should get a clandestine Livelihood but themselves.

SCENE X.

Mrs. PEACHUM, PEACHUM, POLLY.

Polly. 'Twas only Nimming *Ned*. He brought in a Damask Window-Curtain, a Hoop-Petticoat, a pair of Silver Candlesticks, a Periwig, and one Silk Stocking, from the Fire that happen'd last Night.

Peachum. There is not a Fellow that is cleverer in his way, and saves more Goods out of the Fire than *Ned*. But now, *Polly*, to your Affair; for Matters must not be left as they are. You are married then, it seems?

Polly. Yes, Sir.

Peachum. And how do you propose to live, Child?

Polly. Like other Women, Sir, upon the Industry of my Husband.

Mrs. Peachum. What, is the Wench turn'd Fool?

A Highwayman's Wife, like a Soldier's, hath as little of his Pay, as of his Company.

Peachum. And had not you the common Views of a Gentlewoman in your Marriage, *Polly*?

Polly. I don't know what you mean, Sir.

Peachum. Of a Jointure, and of being a Widow.

Polly. But I love him, Sir; how then could I have Thoughts of parting with him?

Peachum. Parting with him! Why, this is the whole Scheme and Intention of all Marriage Articles. The comfortable Estate of Widow-hood, is the only Hope that keeps up a Wife's Spirits. Where is the Woman who would scruple to be a Wife, if she had it in her Power to be a Widow, whenever she pleas'd? If you have any Views of this sort, *Polly*, I shall think the Match not so very unreasonable.

Polly. How I dread to hear your Advice! Yet I must beg you to explain yourself.

Peachum. Secure what he hath got, have him peach'd the next Sessions, and then at once you are made a rich Widow.

Polly. What, murder the Man I love! The Blood runs cold at my Heart with the very Thought of it!

Peachum. Fie, *Polly*! What hath Murder to do in the Affair? Since the thing sooner or later must happen, I dare say, the Captain himself would like that we should get the Reward for his Death sooner than a Stranger. Why, *Polly*, the Captain knows that as 'tis his Employment to rob, so 'tis ours to take Robbers; every Man in his Business. So that there is no Malice in the Case.

Mrs. Peachum. Ay, Husband, now you have nick'd the Matter. To have him peach'd is the only thing could ever make me forgive her.

AIR XII.—Now ponder well, ye Parents dear.

Polly.
O ponder well! be not severe;
So save a wretched Wife!
For on the Rope that hangs my Dear
Depends poor Polly's *Life.*

Mrs. Peachum. But your Duty to your Parents, Hussy, obliges you to hang him. What would many a Wife give for such an Opportunity!

Polly. What is a Jointure, what is Widow-hood to me? I know my Heart. I cannot survive him.

AIR XIII.—Le printemps rappelle aux armes.

The Turtle thus with plaintive Crying,
Her Lover dying,
The Turtle thus with plaintive Crying,
Laments her Dove.
Down she drops quite spent with Sighing,
Pair'd in Death, as pair'd in Love.

Thus, Sir, it will happen to your poor *Polly.*

Mrs. Peachum. What, is the Fool in Love in earnest then? I hate thee for being particular: Why, Wench, thou art a Shame to thy very Sex.

Polly. But hear me, Mother.——If you ever lov'd——

BEGGAR'S OPERA, ACT III,

as Originally perform'd at Lincolns Inn Fields, 1727.

Performers.

1. Macheath. Mr Walker. 2. Lockitt. Mr Hall. 3. Peachum. Mr Hippisley. 4. Lucy. Mrs Egleton. 5. Polly. Miss Fenton, afterwards Dutchess of Bolton.

Audience.

6. Duke of Bolton. 7. Major Pauncefort. 8. Sir Robert Fagg. 9. Mr Rich, the Manager. 10. Mr Cock, the Auctioneer. 11. Mr Gay. 12. Lady Jane Cook. 13. Anthony Henley Esqr. 14. Lord Gage. 15. Sir Conyers Dr Ivry. 16. Sir Tho.s Robinson.

Publish'd 1 July 1790. by J.R.L. Rezold, Cheapside, & at the Shakspeare Gallery, Pall Mall.

THE BEGGAR'S OPERA, 1727, PERFORMERS AND AUDIENCE

MR. LOWE AND MRS. CHAMBERS AS
MACHEATH AND POLLY

"Fondly let me loll"

Mrs. Peachum. Those cursed Play-Books she reads have been her Ruin. One Word more, Hussy, and I shall knock your Brains out, if you have any.

Peachum. Keep out of the way, *Polly*, for fear of Mischief, and consider of what is propos'd to you.

Mrs. Peachum. Away, Hussy. Hang your Husband, and be dutiful.

SCENE XI.

Mrs. PEACHUM, PEACHUM.

[Polly *listning.*]

Mrs. Peachum. The Thing, Husband, must and shall be done. For the sake of Intelligence we must take other Measures, and have him peach'd the next Session without her Consent. If she will not know her Duty, we know ours.

Peachum. But really, my Dear, it grieves one's Heart to take off a great Man. When I consider his Personal Bravery, his fine Stratagem, how much we have already got by him, and how much more we may get, methinks I can't find in my Heart to have a hand in his Death. I wish you could have made *Polly* undertake it.

Mrs. Peachum. But in a Case of Necessity——— our own Lives are in danger.

Peachum. Then, indeed, we must comply with the Customs of the World, and make Gratitude give way to Interest.———He shall be taken off.

Mrs. Peachum. I'll undertake to manage *Polly.*

Peachum. And I'll prepare Matters for the *Old Baily.*

SCENE XII.

POLLY.

Now I'm a Wretch, indeed.——Methinks I see him already in the Cart, sweeter and more lovely than the Nosegay in his Hand!——I hear the Crowd extolling his Resolution and Intrepidity!——What Vollies of Sighs are sent from the Windows of *Holborn*, that so comely a Youth should be brought to Disgrace!—I see him at the Tree! The whole Circle are in Tears!——even Butchers weep!—— *Jack Ketch* himself hesitates to perform his Duty, and would be glad to lose his Fee, by a Reprieve. What then will become of *Polly*!——As yet I may inform him of their Design, and aid him in his Escape.——It shall be so——But then he flies, absents himself, and I bar myself from his dear dear Conversation! That too will distract me.——If he keep out of the way, my Papa and Mama may in time relent, and we may be happy.——If he stays, he is hang'd, and then he is lost for ever!——He intended to lie conceal'd in my Room, 'till the Dusk of the Evening: If they are abroad, I'll this Instant let him out, lest some Accident should prevent him.

[*Exit and returns.*

SCENE XIII.

POLLY, MACHEATH.

AIR XIV.—Pretty Parrot, say——

Macheath.
Pretty Polly, *say,*
When I was away,
Did your Fancy never stray
To some newer Lover?

Polly.
Without Disguise,
Heaving Sighs,
Doting Eyes,
My constant Heart discover,
Fondly let me loll!

Macheath.
O pretty, pretty Poll.

Polly. And are *you* as fond as ever, my Dear?

Macheath. Suspect my Honour, my Courage, suspect any thing but my Love.——May my Pistols miss Fire, and my Mare slip her Shoulder while I am pursu'd, if I ever forsake thee!

Polly. Nay, my Dear, I have no Reason to doubt you, for I find in the Romance you lent me, none of the great Heroes were ever false in Love.

AIR XV.—Pray, Fair one, be kind——

Macheath.
My Heart was so free,
It rov'd like the Bee,
'Till Polly *my Passion requited;*
I sipt each Flower,
I chang'd ev'ry Hour,
But here ev'ry Flow'r is united.

Polly. Were you sentenced to Transportation, sure, my Dear, you could not leave me behind you ——could you?

Macheath. Is there any Power, any Force that could tear me from thee? You might sooner tear a Pension out of the Hands of a Courtier, a Fee from a Lawyer, a pretty Woman from a Looking-glass, or any Woman from *Quadrille.*——But to tear me from thee is impossible!

AIR XVI.—Over the Hills and far away.

Were I laid on Greenland's *Coast,*
And in my Arms embrac'd my Lass;
Warm amidst eternal Frost,
Too soon the Half Year's Night would pass.

Polly.
Were I sold on Indian *Soil,*
Soon as the burning Day was clos'd,
I could mock the sultry Toil
When on my Charmer's Breast repos'd.

Macheath.   *And I would love you all the Day,*
Polly.   *Every Night would kiss and play,*
Macheath.   *If with me you'd fondly stray*
Polly.   *Over the Hills and far away.*

Polly. Yes, I would go with thee. But oh!——
how shall I speak it? I must be torn from thee.
We must part.
Macheath. How! Part!
Polly. We must, we must.——My Papa and
Mama are set against thy Life. They now, even
now are in Search after thee. They are preparing
Evidence against thee. Thy Life depends upon a
moment.

AIR XVII.——Gin thou wert mine awn thing——

Oh what Pain it is to part!
Can I leave thee, can I leave thee?
O what pain it is to part!
Can thy Polly *ever leave thee?*
But lest Death my Love should thwart,
And bring thee to the fatal Cart,
Thus I tear thee from my bleeding Heart!
Fly hence, and let me leave thee.

One Kiss and then—one Kiss—begone—farewell.
Macheath. My Hand, my Heart, my Dear, is so
riveted to thine, that I cannot unloose my Hold.
Polly. But my Papa may intercept thee, and then
I should lose the very glimmering of Hope. A few

Weeks, perhaps, may reconcile us all.   Shall thy *Polly* hear from thee?

Macheath. Must I then go?

Polly. And will not Absence change your Love?

Macheath. If you doubt it, let me stay—and be hang'd.

Polly. O how I fear! how I tremble!——— Go———but when Safety will give you leave, you will be sure to see me again; for 'till then Polly is wretched.

AIR XVIII.—O the Broom, &c.

[Parting, and looking back at each other with fondness; he at one Door, she at the other.

Macheath.
The Miser thus a Shilling sees,
Which he's oblig'd to pay,
With sighs resigns it by degrees,
And fears 'tis gone for aye.

Polly.
The Boy, thus, when his Sparrow's flown,
The Bird in Silence eyes;
But soon as out of Sight 'tis gone,
Whines, whimpers, sobs and cries.

Dighton del.   Publish'd Augⁿ 26, 1782, by T. Lowndes, & Partners.   Walker sculp.

Mᵣ MATOCKS and Mᵣˢ CARGILL as MACHEATH & POLLY.

Mach. *Must I then go?*
Polly. *And will not absence change your love.*

Tho.ˢ Hudson Pinxit.   A. Van Haecken fecit.

DR. JOHN CHRISTOPHER PEPUSCH

ACT II. SCENE I.

A Tavern near Newgate.

Jemmy Twitcher, *Crook-finger'd* Jack, Wat Dreary, Robin *of* Bagshot, Nimming Ned, Henry Padington, Matt *of the* Mint, Ben Budge, *and the rest of the Gang, at the Table, with Wine, Brandy and Tobacco.*

Ben.

BUT pr'ythee, *Matt*, what is become of thy Brother *Tom?* I have not seen him since my Return from Transportation.

Matt. Poor Brother *Tom* had an Accident this time Twelvemonth, and so clever a made fellow he was, that I could not save him from those fleaing Rascals the Surgeons; and now, poor Man, he is among the Otamys at *Surgeons Hall.*

Ben. So it seems, his Time was come.

Jemmy. But the present Time is ours, and no body alive hath more. Why are the Laws levell'd at us? are we more dishonest than the rest of Mankind?

29

What we win, Gentlemen, is our own by the Law of Arms, and the Right of Conquest.

Crook. Where shall we find such another Set of Practical Philosophers, who to a Man are above the Fear of Death?

Wat. Sound Men, and true!

Robin. Of try'd Courage, and indefatigable Industry!

Ned. Who is there here that would not die for his Friend?

Harry. Who is there here that would betray him for his Interest?

Matt. Show me a Gang of Courtiers that can say as much.

Ben. We are for a just Partition of the World, for every Man hath a Right to enjoy Life.

Matt. We retrench the Superfluities of Mankind. The World is avaritious, and I hate Avarice. A covetous fellow, like a Jackdaw, steals what he was never made to enjoy, for the sake of hiding it. These are the Robbers of Mankind, for Money was made for the Free-hearted and Generous, and where is the Injury of taking from another, what he hath not the Heart to make use of?

Jemmy. Our several Stations for the Day are fixt. Good luck attend us all. Fill the Glasses.

AIR XIX.—Fill every Glass, &c.

Matt.

Fill ev'ry Glass, for Wine inspires us,
And fires us

With Courage, Love and Joy.
Women and Wine should Life employ.
Is there ought else on Earth desirous?

Chorus.
Fill every Glass, &c.

SCENE II.

To them enter MACHEATH.

Macheath. Gentlemen, well met. My Heart hath
been with you this Hour; but an unexpected Affair
hath detain'd me. No Ceremony, I beg you.

Matt. We were just breaking up to go upon
Duty. Am I to have the Honour of taking the Air
with you, Sir, this Evening upon the Heath? I drink
a Dram now and then with the Stage-coachmen in
the way of Friendship and Intelligence; and I know
that about this Time there will be Passengers upon
the Western Road, who are worth speaking with.

Macheath. I was to have been of that Party——
but——

Matt. But what, sir?

Macheath. Is there any Man who suspects my
Courage?

Matt. We have all been Witnesses of it.

Macheath. My Honour and Truth to the Gang?

Matt. I'll be answerable for it.

Macheath. In the Division of our Booty, have I
ever shewn the least Marks of Avarice or Injustice?

Matt. By these Questions something seems to have ruffled you. Are any of us suspected?

Macheath. I have a fixed Confidence, Gentlemen, in you all, as Men of Honour, and as such I value and respect you. *Peachum* is a Man that is useful to us.

Matt. Is he about to play us any foul Play? I'll shoot him through the Head.

Macheath. I beg you, Gentlemen, act with Conduct and Discretion. A Pistol is your last Resort.

Matt. He knows nothing of this Meeting.

Macheath. Business cannot go on without him. He is a Man who knows the World, and is a necessary Agent to us. We have had a slight Difference, and 'till it is accommodated I shall be oblig'd to keep out of his way. Any private Dispute of mine shall be of no ill consequence to my Friends. You must continue to act under his Direction, for the moment we break loose from him, our Gang is ruin'd.

Matt. As a Bawd to a Whore, I grant you, he is to us of great Convenience.

Macheath. Make him believe I have quitted the Gang, which I can never do but with Life. At our private Quarters I will continue to meet you. A Week or so will probably reconcile us.

Matt. Your Instructions shall be observ'd. 'Tis now high time for us to repair to our several Duties; so 'till the Evening at our Quarters in *Moor-Fields* we bid you farewell.

Macheath. I shall wish myself with you. Success attend you.   [*Sits down melancholy at the Table.*

Polly

J. Roberts ad viv. del. 1774

Mrs Colles in the Character of *Polly*

The Beggars Opera.

Sr Robert ad viv delt

Miss Catley in the Clerecter of Polly.

AIR XX.—March in *Rinaldo*, with Drums
and Trumpets.

Matt.

Let us take the Road.
*   Hark ! I hear the Sound of Coaches !*
*   The Hour of Attack approaches,*
To your Arms, brave Boys, and load.

See the Ball I hold !
*   Let the Chymists toil like Asses,*
*   Our Fire their Fire surpasses,*
And turns all our Lead to Gold.

[The Gang, rang'd in the Front of the Stage, load
their Pistols, and stick them under their
Girdles; then go off singing the first Part in
Chorus.

SCENE III.

MACHEATH, DRAWER.

Macheath. What a Fool is a fond Wench ! *Polly*
is most confoundedly bit.—I love the Sex. And a
Man who loves Money, might as well be contented
with one Guinea, as I with one Woman. The Town
perhaps have been as much obliged to me, for re-
cruiting it with free-hearted Ladies, as to any Re-
cruiting Officer in the Army. If it were not for us,
and the other Gentlemen of the Sword, *Drury-Lane*
would be uninhabited.

AIR XXI.—Would you have a young Virgin, &c.

If the Heart of a Man is deprest with Cares,
The Mist is dispell'd when a Woman appears;
Like the Notes of a Fiddle, she sweetly, sweetly
Raises the Spirits, and charms our Ears,
  Roses and Lilies her Cheeks disclose,
  But her ripe Lips are more sweet than those.
      Press her,
      Caress her,
      With Blisses,
      Her Kisses
Dissolve us in Pleasure, and soft Repose.

I must have Women. There is nothing unbends the Mind like them. Money is not so strong a Cordial for the Time. Drawer.—[*Enter Drawer.*] Is the Porter gone for all the Ladies according to my Directions?

Drawer. I expect him back every Minute. But you know, Sir, you sent him as far as *Hockley in the Hole* for three of the Ladies, for one in *Vinegar-Yard* and for the rest of them somewhere about *Lewkner's Lane.* Sure some of them are below, for I hear the Bar-Bell. As they come I will show them up. Coming, Coming.

SCENE IV.

Macheath, *Mrs.* Coaxer, Dolly Trull, *Mrs.* Vixen,
Betty Doxy, Jenny Diver, *Mrs.* Slammekin,
Suky Tawdry, *and* Molly Brazen.

Macheath. Dear Mrs. *Coaxer*, you are welcome.
You look charmingly to-day. I hope you don't
want the Repairs of Quality, and lay on Paint.———
Dolly Trull! kiss me, you Slut; are you as amorous
as ever, Hussy? You are always so taken up with
stealing Hearts, that you don't allow yourself Time
to steal anything else.———Ah *Dolly*, thou wilt ever
be a Coquette!———Mrs. *Vixen*, I'm yours, I always
lov'd a Woman of Wit and Spirit; they make charm-
ing Mistresses, but plaguy Wives.———*Betty Doxy!*
Come hither, Hussy. Do you drink as hard as ever?
You had better stick to good wholesom Beer; for in
troth, *Betty*, Strong-Waters will in time ruin your
Constitution. You should leave those to your
Betters.—What! and my pretty *Jenny Diver* too!
As prim and demure as ever! There is not any
Prude, though ever so high bred, hath a more
sanctify'd Look, with a more mischievous Heart.
Ah! thou art a dear artful Hypocrite.———Mrs.
Slammekin! as careless and genteel as ever! all you
fine Ladies, who know your own Beauty, affect an
Undress.———But see, here's *Suky Tawdry* come to
contradict what I was saying. Everything she gets
one way she lays out upon her Back. Why, *Suky*,

you must keep at least a Dozen Tallymen. *Molly Brazen!* [*She kisses him.*] That's well done. I love a free-hearted Wench. Thou hast a most agreeable Assurance, Girl, and art as willing as a Turtle.———— But hark! I hear Music. The Harper is at the Door. *If Music be the Food of Love, play on.* Ere you seat yourselves, Ladies, what think you of a Dance? Come in. [*Enter Harper.*] Play the *French* Tune, that Mrs. *Slammekin* was so fond of.

[*A dance* a la ronde *in the* French *manner; near the end of it this Song and Chorus.*

AIR XXII.—Cotillon.

Youth's the Season made for Joys,
*   Love is then our Duty,*
She alone who that employs,
*   Well deserves her Beauty.*
*   Let's be gay,*
*   While we may,*
*   Beauty's a Flower, despis'd in Decay,*
Youth's the Season, &c.

Let us drink and sport to-day,
*   Ours is not to-morrow.*
Love with youth flies swift away,
*   Age is nought but Sorrow.*
*   Dance and sing,*
*   Time's on the Wing.*
*   Life never knows the Return of Spring.*
Chorus. *Let us drink, &c.*

Macheath. Now, pray Ladies, take your Places. Here Fellow. [*Pays the Harper.*] Bid the Drawer bring us more Wine. [*Exit Harper.*] If any of the Ladies choose Ginn, I hope they will be so free to call for it.

Jenny. You look as if you meant me. Wine is strong enough for me. Indeed, Sir, I never drink Strong-Waters, but when I have the Cholic.

Macheath. Just the Excuse of the fine Ladies! Why, a Lady of Quality is never without the Cholic. I hope, Mrs. *Coaxer*, you have had good Success of late in your Visits among the Mercers.

Coaxer. We have so many interlopers——Yet with Industry, one may still have a little Picking. I carried a silver-flower'd Lutestring, and a Piece of black Padesoy to Mr. *Peachum*'s Lock but last Week.

Vixen. There's *Molly Brazen* hath the Ogle of a Rattle-Snake. She rivitted a Linen-Draper's Eye so fast upon her, that he was nick'd of three Pieces of Cambric before he could look off.

Brazen. Oh dear Madam!——But sure nothing can come up to your handling of Laces! And then you have such a sweet deluding Tongue! To cheat a Man is nothing; but the Woman must have fine Parts indeed who cheats a Woman.

Vixen. Lace, Madam, lies in a small Compass, and is of easy Conveyance. But you are apt, Madam, to think too well of your Friends.

Coaxer. If any woman hath more Art than another, to be sure, 'tis *Jenny Diver*. Though her Fellow be never so agreeable, she can pick his Pocket as coolly, as if money were her only Pleasure. Now that is a Command of the Passions uncommon in a Woman!

Jenny. I never go to the Tavern with a Man, but in the View of Business. I have other Hours, and other sort of Men for my Pleasure. But had I your Address, Madam——

Macheath. Have done with your Compliments, Ladies; and drink about: You are not so fond of me, *Jenny*, as you used to be.

Jenny. 'Tis not convenient, Sir, to shew my Fondness among so many Rivals. 'Tis your own Choice, and not the Warmth of my Inclination that will determine you.

AIR XXIII.—All in a misty Morning, &c.

Before the Barn-Door crowing,
The Cock by Hens attended,
His Eyes around him throwing,
Stands for a while suspended.
Then One he singles from the Crew,
And cheers the happy Hen;
With how do you do, and how do you do,
And how do you do again.

Macheath. Ah *Jenny*! thou art a dear Slut.
Trull. Pray, Madam, were you ever in keeping?
Tawdry. I hope, Madam, I han't been so long upon the Town, but I have met with some good-fortune as well as my Neighbours.

J.Ellys Pinx.   J.Faber Fecit 1728.

MISS FENTON AS POLLY PEACHUM

DR. ARNE

Trull. Pardon me, Madam, I meant no harm by the Question; 'Twas only in the way of Conversation.

Tawdry. Indeed, Madam, if I had not been a Fool, I might have liv'd very handsomely with my last Friend. But upon his missing five Guineas, he turn'd me off. Now I never suspected he had counted them.

Slammekin. Who do you look upon, Madam, as your best sort of Keepers?

Trull. That, Madam, is thereafter as they be.

Slammekin. I, Madam, was once kept by a *Jew*; and bating their Religion, to Women they are a good sort of People.

Tawdry. Now for my Part, I own I like an old Fellow: For we always make them pay for what they can't do.

Vixen. A spruce Prentice, let me tell you, Ladies, is no ill thing, they bleed freely. I have sent at least two or three Dozen of them in my time to the Plantations.

Jenny. But to be sure, Sir, with so much Good-fortune as you have had upon the Road, you must be grown immensely rich.

Macheath. The Road, indeed, hath done me Justice, but the Gaming-Table hath been my Ruin.

AIR XXIV.—When once I lay with another
Man's Wife, &c.

Jenny.
The Gamesters and Lawyers are Jugglers alike,
  If they meddle, your all is in Danger.
Like Gypsies, if once they can finger a Souse,
Your Pockets they pick, and they pilfer your House
  And give your Estate to a Stranger.

A Man of Courage should never put any thing to
the Risque but his Life. These are the Tools of a
Man of Honour. Cards and Dice are only fit for
cowardly Cheats, who prey upon their Friends.
    [*She takes up his Pistol.* Tawdry *takes up the
        other.*
    Tawdry. This, Sir, is fitter for your Hand. Be-
sides your Loss of Money, 'tis a Loss to the Ladies.
Gaming takes you off from Women. How fond
could I be of you! but before Company 'tis ill
bred.
    Macheath. Wanton Hussies!
    Jenny. I must and will have a Kiss to give my
Wine a Zest.
    [*They take him about the Neck and make signs
        to* Peachum *and Constables, who rush in
        upon him.*

SCENE V.

To them, PEACHUM and Constables.
Peachum. I seize you, Sir, as my Prisoner.
Macheath. Was this well done, *Jenny*?——
Women are Decoy Ducks; who can trust them!
Beasts, Jades, Jilts, Harpies, Furies, Whores!
Peachum. Your Case, Mr. *Macheath*, is not
particular. The greatest Heroes have been ruin'd
by Women. But, to do them Justice, I must own
they are a pretty sort of Creatures, if we could trust
them. You must now, Sir, take your Leave of the
Ladies, and if they have a mind to make you a
Visit, they will be sure to find you at home. This
Gentleman, Ladies, lodges in *Newgate*. Constables,
wait upon the Captain to his Lodgings.

AIR XXV.——When first I laid Siege to my
Chloris, &c.

Macheath.
At the Tree I shall suffer with Pleasure,
At the Tree I shall suffer with Pleasure,
Let me go where I will,
In all kinds of Ill,
I shall find no such Furies as these are.

Peachum. Ladies, I'll take care the Reckoning
shall be discharg'd.
[*Exit* Macheath, *guarded with* Peachum *and*
Constables.

SCENE VI.

The Women remain.

Vixen. Look ye, Mrs. *Jemmy*, though Mr. *Peachum* may have made a private Bargain with you and *Suky Tawdry* for betraying the Captain, as we were all assisting, we ought all to share alike.

Coaxer. I think Mr. *Peachum*, after so long an Acquaintance, might have trusted me as well as *Jenny Diver*.

Slammekin. I am sure at least three Men of his hanging, and in a Year's time too, (if he did me Justice) should be set down to my Account.

Trull. Mrs. *Slammekin*, that is not fair. For you know one of them was taken in Bed with me.

Jenny. As far as a Bowl of Punch or a Treat, I believe Mrs. *Suky* will join with me.——As for any thing else, Ladies, you cannot in Conscience expect it.

Slammekin. Dear Madam——

Trull. I would not for the World——

Slammekin. 'Tis impossible for me——

Trull. As I hope to be sav'd, Madam——

Slammekin. Nay, then, I must stay here all Night——

Trull. Since you command me.

[*Exeunt with great Ceremony.*

SCENE VII.

Newgate.

LOCKIT, Turnkeys, *MACHEATH*, Constables.

Lockit. Noble Captain, you are welcome. You have not been a Lodger of mine this Year and half. You know the Custom, Sir. Garnish, Captain, Garnish. Hand me down those Fetters there.

Macheath. Those, Mr. *Lockit*, seem to bc the heaviest of the whole Set. With your Leave, I should like the further Pair better.

Lockit. Look ye, Captain, we know what is fittest for our Prisoners. When a Gentleman uses me with Civility, I always do the best I can to please him.—— -Hand them down I say.——We have them of all Prices, from one Guinea to ten, and 'tis fitting every Gentleman should please himself.

Macheath. I understand you, Sir. [*Gives Money.*] The Fees here are so many, and so exorbitant, that few Fortunes can bear the Expense of getting off handsomely, or of dying like a Gentleman.

Lockit. Those, I see, will fit the Captain better —Take down the further Pair. Do but examine them, Sir—Never was better work.——How genteely they are made !——They will fit as easy as a Glove, and the nicest Man in *England* might not be asham'd to wear them. [*He puts on the Chains.*] If I had the best Gentleman in the Land in my Custody I could not equip him more handsomely. And so, Sir—I now leave you to your private Meditations.

SCENE VIII.

MACHEATH.

AIR XXVI.—Courtiers, Courtiers, think it no
Harm, &c.

Man may escape from Rope and Gun ;
Nay, some have outliv'd the Doctor's Pill ;
Who takes a Woman must be undone,
    That Basilisk is sure to kill.
The Fly that sips Treacle is lost in the Sweets,
So he that tastes Woman, Woman, Woman,
    He that tastes Woman, ruin meets.

To what a woful Plight have I brought myself!
Here must I (all Day long, 'till I am hang'd) be
confin'd to hear the Reproaches of a Wench who
lays her Ruin at my Door——I am in the Custody
of her Father, and to be sure, if he knows of the
matter, I shall have a fine time on't betwixt this
and my Execution.——But I promis'd the Wench
Marriage——What signifies a Promise to a Woman?
Does not Man in Marriage itself promise a hundred
things that he never means to perform? Do all we
can, Women will believe us; for they look upon a
Promise as an Excuse for following their own In-
clinations.——But here comes *Lucy*, and I cannot
get from her.——Wou'd I were deaf!

SCENE IX.

MACHEATH, LUCY.

Lucy. You base Man you,——how can you look me in the Face after what hath passed between us? ——See here, perfidious Wretch, how I am forc'd to bear about the Load of Infamy you have laid upon me——O *Macheath*! thou hast robb'd me of my Quiet——to see thee tortur'd would give me Pleasure.

AIR XXVII.——A lovely Lass to a Friar came, &c.

Thus when a good Housewife sees a Rat
In her Trap in the Morning taken,
With Pleasure her Heart goes pit-a-pat,
In Revenge for her Loss of Bacon.
Then she throws him
To the Dog or Cat
To be worried, crush'd and shaken.

Macheath. Have you no Bowels, no Tenderness, my dear *Lucy*, to see a Husband in these Circumstances?

Lucy. A Husband!

Macheath. In ev'ry Respect but the Form, and that, my Dear, may be said over us at any time. ——Friends should not insist upon Ceremonies. From a Man of Honour, his Word is as good as his Bond,

Lucy. 'Tis the Pleasure of all you fine Men to insult the Women you have ruin'd.

AIR XXVIII.—'Twas when the Sea was roaring, &c.

How cruel are the Traitors,
  Who lye and swear in jest,
To cheat unguarded Creatures
  Of Virtue, Fame and Rest !
Whoever steals a Shilling,
  Through Shame the Guilt conceals :
In Love the perjur'd Villain
  With Boasts the Theft reveals.

Macheath. The very first Opportunity, my Dear, (have but Patience) you shall be my Wife in whatever manner you please.

Lucy. Insinuating Monster ! And so you think I know nothing of the Affair of Miss *Polly Peachum*.——I could tear thy Eyes out !

Macheath. Sure, *Lucy*, you can't be such a Fool as to be jealous of *Polly* !

Lucy. Are you not married to her, you Brute, you.

Macheath. Married ! Very good. The Wench gives it out only to vex thee, and to ruin me in thy good Opinion. 'Tis true, I go to the House; I chat with the Girl, I kiss her, I say a thousand things to her (as all Gentlemen do) that mean nothing, to divert myself; and now the silly Jade hath set it about that I am married to her, to let

me know what she would be at. Indeed, my dear
Lucy, these violent Passions may be of ill consequence to a Woman in your Condition.

Lucy. Come, come, Captain, for all your Assurance, you know that Miss *Polly* hath put it out of
your Power to do me the Justice you promis'd me.

Macheath. A jealous Woman believes everything
her Passion suggests. To convince you of my Sincerity, if we can find the Ordinary, I shall have no
Scruples of making you my Wife; and I know the
Consequence of having two at a time.

Lucy. That you are only to be hang'd, and so
get rid of them both.

Macheath. I am ready, my dear *Lucy*, to give
you Satisfaction——if you think there is any in
Marriage.——What can a Man of Honour say
more?

Lucy. So then, it seems, you are not married to
Miss *Polly*.

Macheath. You know, *Lucy*, the Girl is pro-
digiously conceited. No Man can say a civil thing
to her, but (like other fine Ladies) her Vanity makes
her think he's her own for ever and ever.

AIR XXIX.—The Sun had loos'd his weary
Teams, &c.

The first time at the Looking-glass
The Mother sets her Daughter,
The Image strikes the smiling Lass
With Self-love ever after,

Each time she looks, she, fonder grown,
Thinks ev'ry Charm grows stronger.
But alas, vain Maid, all Eyes but your own
Can see you are not younger.

When Women consider their own Beauties, they
are all alike unreasonable in their Demands; for
they expect their Lovers should like them as long
as they like themselves.

Lucy. Yonder is my Father——perhaps this way
we may light upon the Ordinary, who shall try if
you will be as good as your Word.——For I long to
be made an honest Woman.

———————————————————————
———————————————————————

SCENE X.

PEACHUM, LOCKIT with an Account-Book.

Lockit. In this last Affair, Brother *Peachum*, we
are agreed. You have consented to go halves in
Macheath.

Peachum. We shall never fall out about an
Execution——But as to that Article, pray how
stands our last Year's Account?

Lockit. If you will run your Eye over it, you'll
find 'tis fair and clearly stated.

Peachum. This long Arrear of the Government
is very hard upon us! Can it be expected that we
would hang our Acquaintance for nothing, when
our Betters will hardly save theirs without being
paid for it. Unless the People in Employment pay

THE BEGGAR'S OPERA BURLESQUED (HOGARTH)

1727. Monday Jan^ry 29th Beggars Opera 1st Day (By Mr Gay)

Wriosglow Wilno — 22 — 10 — 0
Redfern — 12 — 0 — 0   D. of Lancaster
Lawrence — 11 — 10 — 0
Taylor — 8 — 5 — 0   Coll. Townshend
Atkins — 7 — 10 — 0   Sr Clem^t Cotterll

———————
61 — 15 — 0

Rogas — 1 — 15 — 0

Stage — 2 — 0 — 0

Gwin 142 ⎫
Pitt 307 ⎩ Gedlant 157 ⎰ 45 — 3 — 0 ⎰ Mr Quin.
from ye Box — 0 — 2 — 0 ⎭

Shafto 28   2 — 16 — 0
Jubman 24   2 — 8 — 0   Lady Oxford Maun Mr Gordon Clack
Slips Roger — 0 — 8 — 0   Mr J. Rich 2 Mr Chr. Rich

Fr. Gall. 437 ⎰ 43 — 14 — 0 Notts Mr J. Rich 2 Ord^rs Mr J. Rich 2.
Mr Cutridge. Mr J. Rich. Mc Luridge.

upp^r G 191 — 9 — 11 — 0

Tot — 169 — 12 — 0

Ord^rs
3 Box.s — 0 — 15 — 0
1 Pitt — 0 — 3 — 0
5 Slips — 0 — 10 — 0
7 Fr. Gall — 0 — 14 — 0
— upp^r G — 0 — 0 — 0
———————
7 — 14 — 0
2 — 02 — 0

Ex.

RECEIPTS OF FIRST DAY

better, I promise them for the future, I shall let other Rogues live besides their own.

Lockit. Perhaps, Brother, they are afraid these Matters may be carried too far. We are treated too by them with Contempt, as if our Profession were not reputable.

Peachum. In one respect indeed our Employment may be reckon'd dishonest, because, like Great Statesmen, we encourage those who betray their Friends.

Lockit. Such Language, Brother, any where else, might turn to your Prejudice. Learn to be more guarded, I beg you.

AIR XXX.—How happy are we, &c.

When you censure the Age,
Be cautious and sage,
Lest the Courtiers offended should be:
If you mention Vice or Bribe,
'Tis so pat to all the Tribe;
Each cries——That was levell'd at me.

Peachum. Here's poor *Ned Clincher's* Name, I see. Sure, Brother *Lockit*, there was a little unfair Proceeding in *Ned's* Case: for he told me in the Condemn'd Hold, that for Value receiv'd, you had promis'd him a Session or two longer without Molestation.

Lockit. Mr. *Peachum*——this is the first time my Honour was ever call'd in Question.

Peachum. Business is at an end—if once we act dishonourably.

Lockit. Who accuses me?

Peachum. You are warm, Brother.

Lockit. He that attacks my Honour, attacks my Livelihood——And this Usage——Sir——is not to be borne.

Peachum. Since you provoke me to speak—I must tell you too, that Mrs. *Coaxer* charges you with defrauding her of her Information-Money, for the apprehending of curl-pated *Hugh*. Indeed, indeed, Brother, we must punctually pay our Spies, or we shall have no Information.

Lockit. Is this Language to me, Sirrah,——who have sav'd you from the Gallows, Sirrah !

[*Collaring each other.*

Peachum. If I am hang'd, it shall be for ridding the World of an arrant Rascal.

Lockit. This Hand shall do the Office of the Halter you deserve, and throttle you——you Dog !——

Peachum. Brother, Brother——We are both in the Wrong——We shall be both Losers in the Dispute——for you know we have it in our Power to hang each other. You should not be so passionate.

Lockit. Nor you so provoking.

Peachum. 'Tis our mutual Interest; 'tis for the Interest of the World we should agree. If I said any thing, Brother, to the Prejudice of your Character, I ask pardon.

Lockit. Brother *Peachum*——I can forgive as

well as resent.——Give me your Hand. Suspicion does not become a Friend.

Peachum. I only meant to give you Occasion to justify yourself. But I must now step home, for I expect the Gentleman about this Snuff-box, that *Filch* nimm'd two Nights ago in the Park. I appointed him at this Hour.

SCENE XI.

LOCKIT, LUCY.

Lockit. Whence come you, Hussy?

Lucy. My Tears might answer that Question.

Lockit. You have then been whimpering and fondling, like a Spaniel, over the Fellow that hath abus'd you.

Lucy. One can't help Love; one can't cure it. 'Tis not in my Power to obey you, and hate him.

Lockit. Learn to bear your Husband's Death like a reasonable Woman. 'Tis not the fashion, now-a-days, so much as to affect Sorrow upon these Occasions. No Woman would ever marry, if she had not the Chance of Mortality for a Release. Act like a Woman of Spirit, Hussy, and thank your Father for what he is doing.

AIR XXXI.—Of a noble Race was *Shenkin.*

Lucy.

Is then his Fate decreed, Sir?

Such a Man can I think of quitting?

When first we met, so moves me yet,
O see how my Heart is splitting!

Lockit. Look ye, *Lucy*—There is no saving him
——So, I think, you must ev'n do like other
Widows——buy yourself Weeds, and be cheerful.

AIR XXXII.

You'll think ere many Days ensue
This Sentence not severe;
I hang your Husband, Child, 'tis true,
But with him hang your Care.
Twang dang dillo dee.

Like a good Wife, go moan over your dying
Husband. That, Child, is your Duty—Consider,
Girl, you can't have the Man and the Money too—
so make yourself as easy as you can, by getting all
you can from him.

SCENE XII.

LUCY, MACHEATH.

Lucy. Though the Ordinary was out of the way
to-day, I hope, my Dear, you will, upon the first
Opportunity, quiet my Scruples——Oh Sir!——
my Father's hard heart is not to be soften'd, and I
am in the utmost Despair.

Macheath. But if I could raise a small Sum——

Mr Vernon in the Character of Macheath.

This best friend a brimmer

Air LIX.

Publish'd by I. Wenman 1st Dec.r 1776.

J.Roberts del.   Publish'd for Bells British Theatre Feb 2 1777   Ja.ˢ Roberts sculp

Mᴿ VERNON in the Character of MACKHEATH.

If thus a Man can Die,

Much bolder with Brandy.

Would not twenty Guineas, think you, move him?
——Of all the Arguments in the way of Business,
the Perquisite is the most prevailing——Your
Father's Perquisites for the Escape of Prisoners
must amount to a considerable Sum in the Year.
Money well tim'd, and properly apply'd, will do
anything.

AIR XXXIII.—*London* Ladies.

If you at an Office solicit your Due,
  And would not have Matters neglected;
You must quicken the Clerk with the Perquisite too,
  To do what his Duty directed.
Or would you the Frowns of a Lady prevent,
  She too has this palpable Failing,
The Perquisite softens her into Consent;
  That Reason with all is prevailing.

Lucy. What Love or Money can do shall be
done: for all my Comfort depends upon your
Safety.

SCENE XIII.

LUCY, MACHEATH, POLLY.

Polly. Where is my dear Husband?——Was a
Rope ever intended for this Neck!——O let me
throw my Arms about it, and throttle thee with

Love!——Why dost thou turn away from me?
——'Tis thy *Polly*——'Tis thy Wife.

Macheath. Was ever such an unfortunate Rascal as I am!

Lucy. Was there ever such another Villain!

Polly. O *Macheath*! was it for this we parted? Taken! Imprison'd! Try'd! Hang'd—cruel Reflection! I'll stay with thee 'till Death—no Force shall tear thy dear Wife from thee now.——What means my Love?——Not one kind Word! not one kind Look! think what thy *Polly* suffers to see thee in this Condition.

AIR XXXIV.—All in the Downs, &c.

Thus when the Swallow, seeking Prey,
  Within the Sash is closely pent,
His Comfort, with bemoaning Lay,
  Without sits pining for th' Event.
Her chatt'ring Lovers all around her skim;
She heeds them not (poor Bird!) her Soul's with him.

Macheath. I must disown her. [*Aside.*] The Wench is distracted.

Lucy. Am I then bilk'd of my Virtue? Can I have no Reparation? Sure Men were born to lie, and Women to believe them! O Villain! Villain!

Polly. Am I not thy Wife?——Thy Neglect of me, thy Aversion to me too severely proves it.—— Look on me.——Tell me, am I not thy Wife?

Lucy. Perfidious Wretch!

Polly. Barbarous Husband!

Lucy. Hadst thou been hang'd five Months ago, I had been happy.

Polly. And I too——If you had been kind to me 'till Death, it would not have vexed me——And that's no very unreasonable Request, (though from a Wife) to a Man who hath not above seven or eight Days to live.

Lucy. Art thou then married to another? Hast thou two Wives, Monster?

Macheath. If Women's Tongues can cease for an Answer——hear me.

Lucy. I won't.—Flesh and Blood can't bear my Usage.

Polly. Shall I not claim my own? Justice bids me speak.

AIR XXXV.—Have you heard of a frolicksome Ditty, &c.

Macheath.
How happy could I be with either,
Were t'other dear Charmer away!
But while you thus teaze me together,
To neither a Word will I say;
But tol de rol, &c.

Polly. Sure, my Dear, there ought to be some Preference shewn to a Wife! At least she may claim the Appearance of it. He must be distracted with his Misfortunes, or he could not use me thus.

Lucy. O Villain, Villain! thou hast deceiv'd me ——I could even inform against thee with Pleasure. Not a Prude wishes more heartily to have Facts against her intimate Acquaintance than I now wish to have Facts against thee. I would have her Satisfaction, and they should all out.

AIR XXXVI.—Irish Trot.

Polly. I am bubbled.
Lucy.   I'm bubbled.
Polly. O how I am troubled!
Lucy. Bambouzled, and bit!
Polly.   My Distresses are doubled.
*Lucy. When you come to the Tree should the
              Hangman refuse,
         These Fingers, with Pleasure, could fasten
              the Noose.*
Polly. I'm bubbled, &c.

Macheath. Be pacified, my dear *Lucy*——This is all a Fetch of *Polly's*, to make me desperate with you in case I get off. If I am hang'd, she would fain have the Credit of being thought my Widow ——Really, *Polly*, this is no time for a Dispute of this sort; for whenever you are talking of Marriage, I am thinking of Hanging.

Polly. And hast thou the Heart to persist in disowning me?

Macheath. And hast thou the Heart to persist in persuading me that I am married? Why, *Polly*, dost thou seek to aggravate my Misfortunes?

CAPTAIN MACHEATH, LUCY AND POLLY

Lucy. Really, Miss *Peachum*, you but expose yourself. Besides, 'tis barbarous in you to worry a Gentleman in his Circumstances.

AIR XXXVII.

Polly.
Cease your Funning;
Force or Cunning
Never shall my Heart trapan.
All these Sallies
Are but Malice
To seduce my constant Man.
'Tis most certain,
By their flirting
Women oft have Envy shown
Pleas'd, to ruin
Others wooing;
Never happy in their own!

Polly. Decency, Madam, methinks might teach you to behave yourself with some Reserve with the Husband, while his Wife is present.

Macheath. But seriously, *Polly*, this is carrying the Joke a little too far.

Lucy. If you are determin'd, Madam, to raise a Disturbance in the Prison, I shall be oblig'd to send for the Turnkey to shew you the Door. I am sorry, Madam, you force me to be so ill-bred.

Polly. Give me leave to tell you, Madam: These forward Airs don't become you in the least,

Madam. And my Duty, Madam, obliges me to stay with my Husband, Madam.

AIR XXXVIII.—Good-morrow, Gossip *Joan.*

Lucy.
Why how now, Madam Flirt?
If you thus must chatter;
And are for flinging Dirt,
    Let's try who best can spatter;
                Madam Flirt!

Polly.
Why how now, saucy Jade;
    Sure the Wench is tipsy!
How can you see me made   [To him.
    The Scoff of such a Gipsy?
                Saucy Jade! [To her.

SCENE XIV.

LUCY, MACHEATH, POLLY, PEACHUM.

Peachum. Where's my Wench? Ah, Hussy: Hussy!——Come you home, you Slut; and when your Fellow is hang'd, hang yourself, to make your Family some Amends.

Polly. Dear, dear Father, do not tear me from him——I must speak; I have more to say to him

————Oh! twist thy Fetters about me, that he may not haul me from thee!

Peachum. Sure all Women are alike! If ever they commit the Folly, they are sure to commit another by exposing themselves————Away————Not a Word more————You are my Prisoner, now, Hussy.

AIR XXXIX.—Irish Howl.

Polly.
No Power on Earth can e'er divide
The Knot that sacred Love hath ty'd.
When Parents draw against our Mind,
The True-Love's Knot they faster bind,
  Oh, oh ray, oh Amborah— oh, oh, &c.
  [Holding *Macheath*, *Peachum* pulling her.

SCENE XV.

LUCY, MACHEATH.

Macheath. I am naturally compassionate, Wife; so that I could not use the Wench as she deserv'd; which made you at first suspect there was something in what she said.

Lucy. Indeed, my Dear, I was strangely puzzled.

Macheath. If that had been the Case, her Father would never have brought me into this circumstance————No, *Lucy*————I had rather die than be false to thee.

Lucy. How happy am I, if you say this from your Heart! For I love thee so, that I could sooner bear to see thee hang'd than in the Arms of another.

Macheath. But could'st thou bear to see me hang'd?

Lucy. O *Macheath*, I can never live to see that Day.

Macheath. You see, *Lucy*; in the Account of Love you are in my Debt, and you must now be convinc'd, that I rather choose to die than be another's.——Make me, if possible, love thee more, and let me owe my Life to thee——If you refuse to assist me, *Peachum* and your Father will immediately put me beyond all means of Escape.

Lucy. My Father, I know, hath been drinking hard with the Prisoners; and I fancy he is now taking his Nap in his own Room——If I can procure the Keys, shall I go off with thee, my Dear?

Macheath. If we are together, 'twill be impossible to lie conceal'd. As soon as the search begins to be a little cool, I will send to thee——'Till then my Heart is thy Prisoner.

Lucy. Come then, my dear Husband——owe thy Life to me——and though you love me not ——be grateful,——But that *Polly* runs in my Head strangely.

Macheath. A moment of Time may make us unhappy for ever.

AIR XL.—The Lass of *Patie's* Mill, &c.

Lucy.

I like the Fox shall grieve,
  Whose Mate hath left her Side,
Whom Hounds from Morn to Eve,
  Chase o'er the Country wide.
Where can my Lover hide?
  Where cheat the weary Pack?
If Love be not his Guide,
  He never will come back!

Alexand. Grimaldi a Venetian.
much employ'd in workes of gold ornaments on looking glass.
at last stage door keeper to Lincolns Inn playhouse.

ALEXANDER GRIMALDI,
STAGE DOOR-KEEPER IN LINCOLN'S INN PLAYHOUSE

ACT III. SCENE I.

SCENE, *Newgate.*

LOCKIT, LUCY.

Lockit.

TO be sure, Wench, you must have been aiding and abetting to help him to this Escape.

Lucy. Sir, here hath been *Peachum* and his Daughter *Polly*, and to be sure they know the Ways of *Newgate* as well as if they had been born and bred in the Place all their Lives. Why must all your Suspicion light upon me?

Lockit. Lucy, Lucy, I will have none of these shuffling Answers.

Lucy. Well then——if I know any thing of him I wish I may be burnt!

Lockit. Keep your Temper, *Lucy*, or I shall pronounce you guilty.

Lucy. Keep yours, Sir,——I do wish I may be burnt. I do——And what can I say more to convince you?

Lockit. Did he tip handsomely?——How much

63

did he come down with? Come, Hussy, don't cheat your Father; and I shall not be angry with you ———Perhaps, you have made a better Bargain with him than I could have done———How much, my good Girl?

Lucy. You know, Sir, I am fond of him, and would have given Money to have kept him with me.

Lockit. Ah *Lucy*! thy Education might have put thee more upon thy Guard; for a Girl in the Bar of an Ale-house is always besieg'd.

Lucy. Dear Sir, mention not my Education—for 'twas to that I owe my Ruin.

AIR XLI.—If Love's a sweet Passion, &c.

When young at the Bar you first taught me to score,
And bid me be free of my Lips, and no more;
I was kiss'd by the Parson, the Squire, and the Sot.
When the Guest was departed, the Kiss was forgot,
But his Kiss was so sweet, and so closely he prest,
That I languish'd and pin'd till I granted the rest.

If you can forgive me, Sir, I will make a fair Confession, for to be sure he hath been a most barbarous Villain to me.

Lockit. And so you have let him escape, Hussy ———Have you?

Lucy. When a Woman loves; a kind Look, a tender Word can persuade her to any thing——— And I could ask no other Bribe.

Lockit. Thou wilt always be a vulgar Slut, *Lucy.*—If you would not be look'd upon as a Fool, you should never do any thing but upon the foot of Interest. Those that act otherwise are their own Bubbles.

Lucy. But Love, Sir, is a Misfortune that may happen to the most discreet Woman, and in Love we are all Fools alike——Notwithstanding all he swore, I am now fully convinc'd that *Polly Peachum* is actually his Wife.——Did I let him escape (Fool that I was!) to go to her?——*Polly* will wheedle herself into his Money, and then *Peachum* will hang him, and cheat us both.

Lockit. So I am to be ruin'd, because, forsooth, you must be in Love!——a very pretty Excuse!

Lucy. I could murder that impudent happy Strumpet:—I gave him his Life, and that Creature enjoys the Sweets of it.——Ungrateful *Macheath*!

AIR XLII.—South-Sea Ballad.

My Love is all Madness and Folly,
   Alone I lie,
   Toss, tumble, and cry,
What a happy Creature is Polly!
Was e'er such a Wretch as I!
With rage I redden like Scarlet,
That my dear inconstant Varlet,
   Stark blind to my Charms,
   Is lost in the Arms
Of that Jilt, that inveigling Harlot!

Stark blind to my Charms,
Is lost in the Arms
Of that Jilt, that inveigling Harlot!
This, this my Resentment alarms.

Lockit. And so, after all this Mischief, I must stay here to be entertain'd with your Catterwauling, Mistress Puss !——Out of my Sight, wanton Strumpet ! you shall fast and mortify yourself into Reason, with now and then a little handsome Discipline to bring you to your Senses.——Go.

SCENE II.

LOCKIT.

Peachum then intends to outwit me in this Affair; but I'll be even with him.——The Dog is leaky in his Liquor, so I'll ply him that way, get the Secret from him, and turn this Affair to my own Advantage.——Lions, Wolves and Vultures don't live together in Herds, Droves or Flocks.——Of all Animals of Prey, Man is the only sociable one. Every one of us preys upon his Neighbour, and yet we herd together.——*Peachum* is my Companion, my Friend.——According to the Custom of the World, indeed, he may quote thousands of Precedents for cheating me——And shall not I make use of the Privilege of Friendship to make him a Return.

AIR XLIII.—Packington's Pound.

Thus Gamesters united in Friendship are found,
Though they know that their Industry all is a Cheat;
They flock to their Prey at the Dice-Box's Sound,
And join to promote one another's Deceit.
    But if by mishap
    They fail of a Chap,
To keep in their Hands, they each other entrap.
Like Pikes, lank with Hunger, who miss of their
    Ends,
They bite their Companions, and prey on their
    Friends.

Now, *Peachum*, you and I, like honest Tradesmen are to have a fair Trial which of us two can over-reach the other.——*Lucy.*——[*Enter* Lucy.] Are there any of *Peachum's* People now in the House?

Lucy. *Filch*, Sir, is drinking a Quartern of Strong-Waters in the next Room with *Black Moll.*

Lockit. Bid him come to me.

SCENE III.

LOCKIT, FILCH.

Lockit. Why, Boy, thou lookest as if thou wert half starv'd; like a shotten Herring.

Filch. One had need have the Constitution of a Horse to go through the Business.——Since the favourite Child-getter was disabled by a Mishap, I have pick'd up a little Money by helping the Ladies to a Pregnancy against their being call'd down to Sentence.———But if a Man cannot get an honest Livelihood any easier way, I am sure, 'tis what I can't undertake for another Session.

Lockit. Truly, if that great Man should tip off, 'twould be an irreparable Loss. The Vigor and Prowess of a Knight-Errant never sav'd half the Ladies in Distress that he hath done.———But, Boy, canst thou tell me where thy Master is to be found?

Filch. At his Lock,* Sir, at the Crooked Billet.

Lockit. Very well.—I have nothing more with you. [*Ex.* Filch.] I'll go to him there, for I have many important Affairs to settle with him; and in the way of those Transactions, I'll artfully get into his Secret———So that *Macheath* shall not remain a Day longer out of my Clutches.

SCENE IV.—*A Gaming-House.*

MACHEATH in a fine tarnish'd Coat, BEN BUDGE, MATT of the Mint.

Macheath. I am sorry, Gentlemen, the Road was so barren of Money. When my Friends are in Difficulties, I am always glad that my Fortune can be serviceable to them. [*Gives them Money.*] You

---

* A Cant Word, signifying, a Warehouse where stolen Goods are deposited.

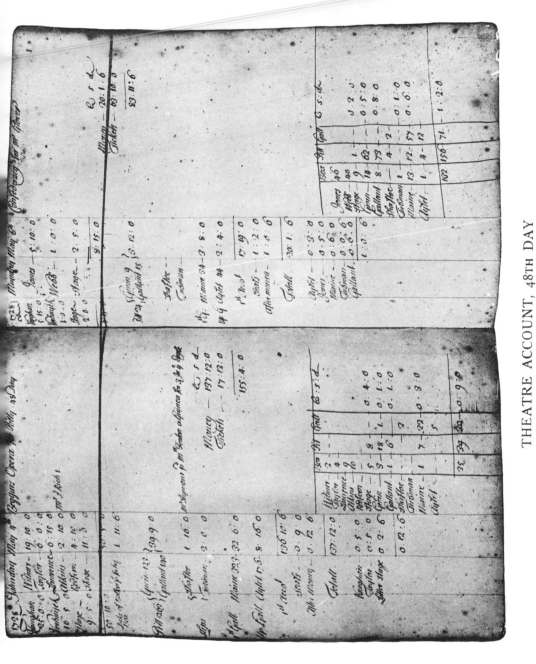

THEATRE ACCOUNT, 48TH DAY

LAVINIA FENTON, AFTERWARDS DUCHESS OF BOLTON

see, Gentlemen, I am not a mere Court Friend, who professes everything and will do nothing.

AIR XLIV.—Lillibullero.

The Modes of the Court so common are grown,
  That a true Friend can hardly be met ;
Friendship for Interest is but a Loan,
  Which they let out for what they can get,
    'Tis true, you find
    Some Friends so kind,
Who will give you good Counsel themselves to defend.
    In sorrowful Ditty,
    They promise, they pity,
But shift you for Money, from Friend to Friend.

But we, Gentlemen, have still Honour enough to break through the Corruptions of the World.——— And while I can serve you, you may command me.

Ben. It grieves my Heart that so generous a Man should be involv'd in such Difficulties, as oblige him to live with such ill Company, and herd with Gamesters.

Matt. See the Partiality of Mankind !——One Man may steal a Horse, better than another look over a Hedge.——Of all Mechanics, of all servile Handicrafts-men, a Gamester is the vilest. But yet, as many of the Quality are of the Profession, he is admitted amongst the politest Company. I wonder we are not more respected.

Macheath. There will be deep Play to-night at

Mary-bone, and consequently Money may be pick'd up upon the Road. Meet me there, and I'll give you the Hint who is worth Setting.

Matt. The Fellow with a brown Coat with a narrow Gold Binding, I am told, is never without Money.

Macheath. What do you mean, *Matt* ?——Sure you will not think of meddling with him !——He's a good honest kind of a Fellow, and one of us.

Ben. To be sure, Sir, we will put ourselves under your Direction.

Macheath. Have an Eye upon the Money-Lenders.——A *Rouleau*, or two, would prove a pretty sort of an Expedition. I hate Extortion.

Matt. Those Rouleaus are very pretty Things.——I hate your Bank Bills.——There is such a Hazard in putting them off.

Macheath. There is a certain Man of Distinction, who in his Time hath nick'd me out of a great deal of the Ready. He is in my Cash, *Ben* ;——I'll point him out to you this Evening, and you shall draw upon him for the Debt.——The Company are met ; I hear the Dice-Box in the other Room. So, Gentlemen, your Servant. You'll meet me at *Mary-bone*.

SCENE V.—*Peachum's Lock.*

A Table with Wine, Brandy, Pipes and Tobacco.

PEACHUM, LOCKIT.

Lockit. The Coronation Account, Brother *Peachum*, is of so intricate a nature, that I believe it will never be settled.

Peachum. It consists indeed of a great Variety of Articles.——It was worth to our People, in Fees of different kinds, above ten Instalments.——This is part of the Account, Brother, that lies open before us.

Lockit. A Lady's Tail of rich Brocade——that, I see, is dispos'd of.

Peachum. To Mrs. *Diana Trapes*, the Tally-Woman, and she will make a good Hand on't in Shoes and Slippers, to trick out young Ladies, upon their going into Keeping——

Lockit. But I don't see any Article of the Jewels.

Peachum. Those are so well known that they must be sent abroad——You'll find them enter'd under the Article of Exportation.——As for the Snuff-Boxes, Watches, Swords, &c.——I thought it best to enter them under their several Heads.

Lockit. Seven and twenty Women's Pockets complete ; with the several things therein contain'd ; all Seal'd, Number'd, and Enter'd.

Peachum. But, Brother, it is impossible for us now to enter upon this Affair.——We should have the whole Day before us.——Besides, the Account of the last Half Year's Plate is in a Book by itself, which lies at the other Office.

Lockit. Bring us then more Liquor.——To-day shall be for Pleasure——To-morrow for Business—— Ah, Brother, those Daughters of ours are two slippery Hussies——Keep a watchful Eye upon *Polly*, and *Macheath* in a Day or two shall be our own again.

AIR XLV.—Down in the North Country, &c.

Lockit.
What Gudgeons are we Men!
    Ev'ry Woman's easy Prey.
Though we have felt the Hook, agen
    We bite and they betray.

The Bird that hath been trapt,
    When he hears his calling Mate,
To her he flies, again he's clapt
    Within the wiry Grate.

Peachum. But what signifies catching the Bird, if your Daughter *Lucy* will set open the Door of the Cage?

Lockit. If Men were answerable for the Follies and Frailties of their Wives and Daughters, no Friends could keep a good Correspondence together for two Days——This is unkind of you, Brother; for among good Friends, what they say or do goes for nothing.

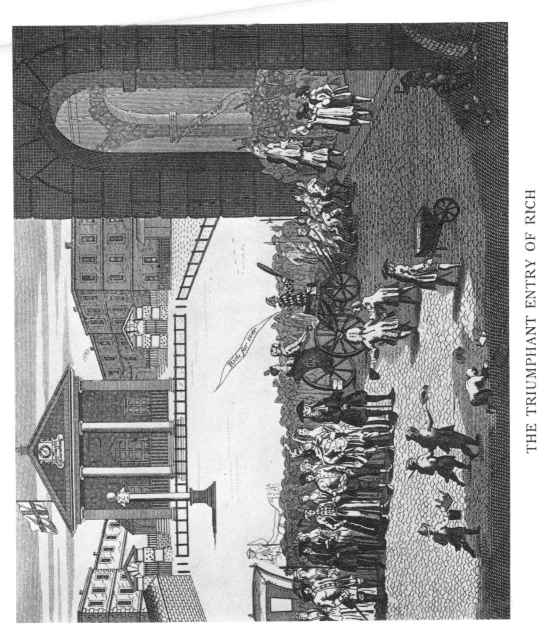

THE TRIUMPHANT ENTRY OF RICH

Enter a Servant.

Servant. Sir, here's Mrs. *Diana Trapes* wants to speak with you.

Peachum. Shall we admit her, Brother *Lockit*?

Lockit. By all means,——She's a good Customer, and a fine-spoken Woman——And a Woman who drinks and talks so freely, will enliven the Conversation.

Peachum. Desire her to walk in. [*Exit Servant.*

SCENE VI.

PEACHUM, LOCKIT, Mrs. TRAPES.

Peachum. Dear Mrs. *Dye*, your Servant—— One may know by your Kiss, that your Ginn is excellent.

Trapes. I was always very curious in my Liquors.

Lockit. There is no perfum'd Breath like it—I have been long acquainted with the Flavour of those Lips—Han't I, Mrs. *Dye*.

Trapes. Fill it up——I take as large Draughts of Liquor, as I did of Love.——I hate a Flincher in either.

AIR XLVI.—A Shepherd kept Sheep, &c.

In the Days of my Youth I could bill like a Dove,
    fa, la, la, &c.
Like a Sparrow at all times was ready for Love,
    fa, la, la, &c.
The Life of all Mortals in Kissing should pass,
Lip to Lip while we're young—then the Lip to the
    Glass, fa, la, &c.

But now, Mr. *Peachum*, to our Business.——If you
have Blacks of any kind, brought in of late; Mantoes
—Velvet Scarfs——Petticoats——Let it be what it
will——I am your Chap——for all my Ladies are
very fond of Mourning.

Peachum. Why, look ye, Mrs. *Dye*——you deal so
hard with us, that we can afford to give the Gentlemen, who venture their Lives for the Goods, little
or nothing.

Trapes. The hard Times oblige me to go very
near in my Dealing.——To be sure, of late Years
I have been a great Sufferer by the Parliament.——
Three thousand Pounds would hardly make me
amends.——The Act for destroying the Mint, was
a severe Cut upon our Business——'Till then, if a
Customer stept out of the way——we knew where
to have her——No doubt you know Mrs. *Coaxer*
——there's a Wench now ('till to-day) with a good
Suit of Clothes of mine upon her Back, and I could
never set Eyes upon her for three Months together.
——Since the Act too against Imprisonment for

small Sums, my Loss there too hath been very considerable, and it must be so, when a Lady can
borrow a handsome Petticoat, or a clean Gown, and
I not have the least Hank upon her! And, o' my
Conscience, now-a-days most Ladies take a Delight
in cheating, when they can do it with Safety.

Peachum. Madam, you had a handsome Gold
Watch of us t'other Day for seven Guineas.————
Considering we must have our Profit————To a
Gentleman upon the Road, a Gold Watch will be
scarce worth the taking.

Trapes. Consider, Mr. *Peachum*, that Watch was
remarkable, and not of very safe Sale.————If you
have any black Velvet Scarfs————they are a handsome Winter-wear, and take with most Gentlemen
who deal with my Customers.————'Tis I that put
the Ladies upon a good Foot. 'Tis not Youth or
Beauty that fixes their Price. The Gentlemen always
pay according to their Dress, from half a Crown to
two Guineas; and yet those Hussies make nothing
of bilking of me.————Then too, allowing for Accid-
ents.————I have eleven fine Customers now down
under the Surgeon's Hands————what with Fees and
other Expenses, there are great Goings-out, and no
Comings in, and not a Farthing to pay for at least
a Month's Clothing.————We run great Risques—
great Risques indeed.

Peachum. As I remember, you said something
just now of Mrs. *Coaxer.*

Trapes. Yes, Sir.————To be sure I stript her of a
Suit of my own Clothes about two Hours ago; and

have left her as she should be, in her Shift, with a Lover of hers at my House. She call'd him up Stairs, as he was going to *Mary-bone* in a Hackney Coach.——And I hope, for her own sake and mine, she will persuade the Captain to redeem her, for the Captain is very generous to the Ladies.

Lockit. What Captain?

Trapes. He thought I did not know him——An intimate Acquaintance of yours, Mr. *Peachum*—— Only Captain *Macheath*——as fine as a Lord.

Peachum. To-morrow, dear Mrs. *Dye*, you shall set your own Price upon any of the Goods you like ——We have at least half a Dozen Velvet Scarfs, and all at your Service. Will you give me leave to make you a Present of this Suit of Night-clothes for your own wearing?——But are you sure it is Captain *Macheath.*

Trapes. Though he thinks I have forgot him; no body knows him better. I have taken a great deal of the Captain's Money in my Time at second-hand, for he always lov'd to have his Ladies well drest.

Peachum. Mr. *Lockit* and I have a little Business with the Captain;——You understand me——and we will satisfy you for Mrs. *Coaxer's* Debt.

Lockit. Depend upon it——we will deal like Men of Honour.

Trapes. I don't enquire after your Affairs——so whatever happens, I wash my Hands on't——It hath always been my Maxim, that one Friend should assist another——But if you please——I'll take one of the Scarfs home with me. 'Tis always good to have somethng in Hand.

SCENE VII.—*Newgate.*
LUCY.

Jealousy, Rage, Love and Fear are at once tearing me to pieces, How I am weather-beaten and shatter'd with Distresses!

AIR XLVII.—One Evening, having lost my Way, &c.

I'm like a Skiff on the Ocean tost,
  Now high, now low, with each Billow born,
With her Rudder broke, and her Anchor lost,
  Deserted and all forlorn.
While thus I lie rolling and tossing all Night,
That Polly *lies sporting on Seas of Delight!*
  Revenge, Revenge, Revenge,
Shall appease my restless Sprite.

I have the Rats-bane ready.——I run no Risque; for I can lay her Death upon the Ginn, and so many die of that naturally that I shall never be call'd in question.——But say, I were to be hang'd.——I never could be hang'd for any thing that would give me greater Comfort, than the poisoning that Slut.

Enter Filch.

Filch. Madam, here's Miss *Polly* come to wait upon you.

Lucy. Show her in.

SCENE VIII.

LUCY, POLLY.

Lucy. Dear Madam, your Servant.——I hope you will pardon my Passion, when I was so happy to see you last.——I was so over-run with the Spleen, that I was perfectly out of myself. And really when one hath the Spleen, everything is to be excus'd by a Friend.

AIR XLVIII.——Now *Roger*, I'll tell thee because thou'rt my Son.

When a Wife's in her Pout,
  (As she's sometimes, no doubt;)
The good Husband as meek as a Lamb,
  Her Vapours to still,
  First grants her her Will,
And the quieting Draught is a Dram.
  Poor Man!
And the quieting Draught is a Dram.

——I wish all our Quarrels might have so comfortable a Reconciliation.

Polly. I have no Excuse for my own Behaviour, Madam, but my Misfortunes.——And really, Madam, I suffer too upon your Account.

Lucy. But, Miss *Polly*——in the way of Friendship, will you give me leave to propose a Glass of Cordial to you?

Polly. Strong-Waters are apt to give me the Head-Ache——I hope, Madam, you will excuse me.

Lucy. Not the greatest Lady in the Land could have better in her Closet, for her own private drinking.——You seem mighty low in Spirits, my Dear.

Polly. I am sorry, Madam, my Health will not allow me to accept of your Offer——I should not have left you in the rude manner I did when we met last, Madam, had not my Papa haul'd me away so unexpectedly——I was indeed somewhat provok'd, and perhaps might use some Expressions that were disrespectful.—— But really, Madam, the Captain treated me with so much Contempt and Cruelty, that I deserv'd your Pity, rather than your Resentment.

Lucy. But since his Escape, no doubt all Matters are made up again.——Ah *Polly*! *Polly*! 'tis I am the unhappy Wife; and he loves you as if you were only his Mistress.

Polly. Sure, Madam, you cannot think me so happy as to be the object of your Jealousy. ——A Man is always afraid of a Woman who loves him too well——so that I must expect to be neglected and avoided.

Lucy. Then our Cases, my dear *Polly*, are exactly alike. Both of us indeed have been too fond.

AIR XLIX.—O *Bessy Bell.*

Polly. A Curse attend that Woman's Love,
　　　Who always would be pleasing.
Lucy. The Pertness of the billing Dove,
　　　Like Tickling, is but teasing.
Polly. What then in Love can Woman do;
Lucy. If we grow fond they shun us.
Polly. And when we fly them, they pursue:
Lucy. But leave us when they've won us.

Lucy. Love is so very whimsical in both Sexes, that it is impossible to be lasting.——But my Heart is particular, and contradicts my own Observation.

Polly. But really, Mistress *Lucy*, by his last Behaviour, I think I ought to envy you.——When I was forc'd from him, he did not shew the least Tenderness.——But perhaps, he hath a Heart not capable of it.

AIR L.—Would Fate to me *Belinda* give.

Among the Men, Coquets we find,
Who court by turns all Woman-kind;
And we grant all their Hearts desir'd,
When they are flatter'd, and admir'd.

The Coquets of both Sexes are Self-lovers, and that is a Love no other whatever can dispossess. I hear, my dear *Lucy*, our Husband is one of those.

Lucy. Away with these melancholy Reflections,
——indeed, my dear *Polly*, we are both of us a
Cup too low——Let me prevail upon you to accept
of my Offer.

AIR LI.——Come, sweet Lass.

> *Come, sweet Lass,*
> *Let's banish Sorrow*
> *'Till To-morrow;*
> *Come, sweet Lass,*
> *Let's take a chirping Glass.*
> *Wine can clear*
> *The Vapours of Despair*
> *And make us light as Air;*
> *Then drink, and banish Care.*

I can't bear, Child, to see you in such low Spirits.
——And I must persuade you to what I know will
do you good.——I shall now soon be even with
the hypocritical Strumpet.   [*Aside.*

SCENE IX.

POLLY.

All this Wheedling of *Lucy* cannot be for nothing.
——At this time too! when I know she hates me!
——The Dissembling of a Woman is always the
Forerunner of Mischief.——By pouring Strong-

Waters down my Throat, she thinks to pump some Secrets out of me,——I'll be upon my Guard, and won't taste a Drop of her Liquor, I'm resolv'd.

SCENE X.

LUCY, with Strong-Waters. POLLY.

Lucy. Come, Miss *Polly.*

Polly. Indeed, Child, you have given yourself trouble to no purpose.——You must, my Dear, excuse me.

Lucy. Really, Miss *Polly*, you are as squeamishly affected about taking a Cup of Strong-Waters as a Lady before Company. I vow, *Polly*, I shall take it monstrously ill if you refuse me.——Brandy and Men (though Women love them ever so well) are always taken by us with some Reluctance——unless 'tis in private.

Polly. I protest, Madam, it goes against me.—— What do I see ! *Macheath* again in Custody !—— Now every Glimm'ring of Happiness is lost.

[*Drops the Glass of Liquor on the Ground.*

Lucy. Since things are thus, I'm glad the Wench hath escap'd; for by this Event, 'tis plain, she was not happy enough to deserve to be poison'd. [*Aside.*

SCENE XI.

*LOCKIT, MACHEATH, PEACHUM, LUCY,
POLLY.*

Lockit. Set your Heart to rest, Captain.——You
have neither the Chance of Love or Money for
another Escape,——for you are order'd to be call'd
down upon your Trial immediately.

Peachum. Away, Hussies!——This is not a
Time for a Man to be hamper'd with his Wives.
——You see, the Gentleman is in Chains already.

Lucy. O Husband, Husband, my Heart long'd
to see thee; but to see thee thus distracts me!

Polly. Will not my dear Husband look upon his
Polly? Why hadst thou not flown to me for Pro-
tection? with me thou hadst been safe.

AIR LII.——The last time I went o'er the Moor.

Polly. Hither, dear Husband, turn your Eyes.
Lucy.   Bestow one Glance to cheer me.
Polly. Think with that Look, thy Polly dies.
Lucy.   O shun me not——but hear me.
Polly. 'Tis Polly sues.
Lucy.   'Tis Lucy speaks.
Polly.   Is thus true Love requited?
Lucy. My Heart is bursting.
Polly.   Mine too breaks.

Lucy. Must I
Polly.   Must I be slighted?

Macheath. What would you have me say, Ladies?
——You see this Affair will soon be at an end, without my disobliging either of you.

Peachum. But the settling this Point, Captain,
might prevent a Law-Suit between your two
Widows.

AIR LIII.—*Tom Tinker's* my true Love.

Macheath.

Which way shall I turn me——How can I decide?
Wives, the Day of our Death, are as fond as a Bride.
One Wife is too much for most Husbands to hear,
But two at a time there's no mortal can bear.
This way, and that way, and which way I will,
What would comfort the one, t'other Wife would
    take ill.

Polly. But if his own Misfortunes have made him
insensible to mine——A Father sure will be more
compassionate——Dear, dear Sir, sink the material
Evidence, and bring him off at his Trial——*Polly,*
upon her Knees begs it of you.

AIR LIV.—I am a poor Shepherd undone.

When my Hero in Court appears,
    And stands arraign'd for his Life;
Then think of poor Polly's Tears;
    For Ah! poor Polly's his Wife.

MISS WELLER, *as* Polly, *in the* Beggar's Opera

When my Hero in Court appears. Song 210.

Published by J. Bew, 1 June, 1778.

Zinck pinx: W.ᵐ Smith del. et sculp:

JOHANNES GAY.

Life is a jest and all things shew it,
I thought so once, but now I know it.

Published at the Act directs Dec.ᵣ 1ᵗ 1772 by I. Thane Gerrard Street Soho

Like the Sailor he holds up his Hand,
Distrest on the dashing Wave.
To die a dry Death at Land,
Is as bad as a wat'ry Grave.
And alas, poor Polly *!*
Alack, and well-a-day!
Before I was in Love,
Oh! every Month was May.

Lucy. If *Peachum's* Heart is harden'd; sure you, Sir, will have more Compassion on a Daughter. ——I know the Evidence is in your Power.—— How then can you be a Tyrant to me? [*Kneeling.*

AIR LV.—*Ianthe* the lovely, &c.

When he holds up his Hand arraign'd for his Life,
O think of your Daughter, and think I'm his Wife!
What are Cannons, or Bombs, or clashing of Swords?
For Death is more certain by Witnesses Words.
Then nail up their Lips; that dread Thunder allay;
And each Month of my Life will hereafter be May.

Lockit. Macheath's Time is come, *Lucy*——We know our own Affairs, therefore let us have no more Whimpering or Whining.

AIR LVI.—A Cobler there was, &c.

Ourselves, like the Great, to secure a Retreat,
When Matters require it, must give up our Gang:
And good reason why,
Or, instead of the Fry,
Ev'n Peachum *and* I.

Like poor petty Rascals, might hang, hang;
Like poor petty Rascals, might hang.

Peachum. Set your Heart at rest, *Polly.*——Your Husband is to die to-day.——Therefore if you are not already provided, 'tis high time to look about for another. There's Comfort for you, you Slut.

Lockit. We are ready, Sir, to conduct you to the *Old Baily.*

AIR LVII.—Bonny Dundee.

Macheath.

The Charge is prepar'd; the Lawyers are met
The Judges all rang'd (a terrible Show!)
I go, undismay'd.——For Death is a Debt,
A Debt on Demand.——So take what I owe.
Then farewell, my Love——Dear Charmers, adieu.
Contented I die——'Tis the better for you,
Here ends all Disputes the rest of our Lives,
For this way at once I please all my Wives.

Now, Gentlemen, I am ready to attend you.

SCENE XII.

LUCY, POLLY, FILCH

Polly. Follow them, *Filch*, to the Court. And when the Trial is over, bring me a particular Account of his Behaviour, and of everything that happen'd

———You'll find me here with Miss *Lucy*. [*Exit Filch.*] But why is all this Musick?

Lucy. The Prisoners, whose Trials are put off 'till next Session, are diverting themselves.

Polly. Sure there is nothing so charming as Musick! I'm fond of it to Distraction!———But alas!———now, all Mirth seems an Insult upon my affliction.———Let us retire, my dear *Lucy*, and indulge our Sorrows.———The noisy Crew, you see, are coming upon us.   [*Exeunt.*

A Dance of Prisoners in Chains, &c.

SCENE XIII.——*The Condemn'd Hold.*

MACHEATH, in a melancholy Posture.

AIR LVIII.——Happy Groves.

O cruel, cruel, cruel Case!
Must I suffer this Disgrace?

AIR LIX.——Of all the Girls that are so smart.

Of all the Friends in time of Grief,
  When threatening Death looks grimmer,
Not one so sure can bring Relief,
  As this best Friend, a Brimmer.   [Drinks.

AIR LX.—*Britons* strike home.

Since I must swing,—— I scorn, I scorn to wince or whine.   [Rises.

AIR LXI.—Chevy Chase.

But now again my Spirits sink;
I'll raise them high with Wine.
                                    [Drinks a Glass of Wine.

AIR LXII.—To old Sir *Simon* the King.

But Valour the stronger grows,
  The stronger Liquor we'er drinking;
And how can we feel our Woes,
  When we've lost the Trouble of Thinking?
                                    [Drinks.

AIR LXIII.—Joy to Great *Caesar*.

If thus——A Man can die
Much bolder with Brandy.
                                    [Pours out a Bumper of Brandy.

AIR LXIV.—There was an old Woman.

So I drink off this Bumper.——And now I can stand the Test.
And my Comrades shall see, that I die as brave as the Best.   [Drinks.

AIR LXV.—Did you ever hear of a gallant Sailor.

But can I leave my pretty Hussies,
Without one Tear, or tender Sigh?

AIR LXVI.—Why are mine Eyes still flowing.

Their Eyes, their Lips, their Busses
Recall my Love,——Ah must I die!

AIR LXVII.—Green Sleeves.

Since Laws were made for ev'ry Degree,
To curb Vice in others, as well as me,
I wonder we han't better Company,
    Upon Tyburn *Tree!*
But Gold from Law can take out the Sting;
And if rich Men like us were to swing,
'Twould thin the Land, such Numbers to string
    Upon Tyburn *Tree!*

Jailor. Some Friends of yours, Captain, desire
to be admitted——I leave you together.

SCENE XIV.

MACHEATH, BEN BUDGE, MATT of the
Mint.

Macheath. For my having broke Prison, you see,
Gentlemen, I am order'd immediate Execution.——
The Sheriff's Officers, I believe, are now at the
Door.——That *Jemmy Twitcher* should peach me,
I own surpris'd me!——'Tis a plain Proof that the
World is all alike, and that even our Gang can no
more trust one another than other People. There-
fore, I beg you, Gentlemen, look well to yourselves,

for in all probability you may live some Months longer.

Matt. We are heartily sorry, Captain, for your Misfortune.——But 'tis what we must all come to.

Macheath. *Peachum* and *Lockit*, you know, are infamous Scoundrels. Their Lives are as much in your Power, as yours are in theirs.——Remember your dying Friend!——'Tis my last Request.—— Bring those Villains to the Gallows before you, and I am satisfied.

Matt. We'll do't.

Jailor. Miss *Polly* and Miss *Lucy* intreat a Word with you.

Macheath. Gentlemen, adieu.

SCENE XV.

LUCY, MACHEATH, POLLY.

Macheath. My dear *Lucy*——My dear *Polly* ——Whatsoever hath pass'd between us is now at an end——If you are fond of marrying again, the best Advice I can give you is to Ship yourselves off for the *West-Indies*, where you'll have a fair Chance of getting a Husband a-piece, or by good Luck, two or three, as you like best.

Polly. How can I support this Sight!

Lucy. There is nothing moves one so much as a great Man in Distress.

AIR LXVIII.—All you that must take a Leap, &c.

Lucy. Would I might be hang'd !
Polly.   And I would so too!
Lucy. To be hang'd with you.
Polly.   My Dear, with you.
Macheath. O leave me to Thought ! I fear ! I
*   doubt !*
I tremble! I droop !——See, my Courage is out.
                    [Turns up the empty Bottle.
Polly. No Token of Love ?
Macheath.   See, my Courage is out.
                    [Turns up the empty Pot.
Lucy. No Token of Love ?
Polly.   Adieu.
Lucy.   Farewell.
Macheath. But hark ! I hear the Toll of the
*   Bell.*
Chorus.   Tol de rol lol, &c.

Jailor. Four Women more, Captain, with a
Child apiece ! See, here they come.
                    [*Enter Women and Children.*
Macheath. What——four Wives more !——This
is too much——Here——tell the Sheriff's Officers
I am ready.   [*Exit* Macheath *guarded.*

SCENE XVI.

To them, Enter PLAYER and BEGGAR.

Player. But, honest Friend, I hope you don't intend that *Macheath* shall be really executed.

Beggar. Most certainly, Sir.——To make the
Piece perfect, I was for doing strict poetical Justice
——*Macheath* is to be hang'd; and for the other
Personages of the Drama, the Audience must have
suppos'd they were all either hang'd or transported.

Player. Why then, Friend, this is a downright deep
Tragedy. The Catastrophe is manifestly wrong, for
an Opera must end happily.

Beggar. Your Objection, Sir, is very just, and is
easily remov'd. For you must allow, that in this
kind of Drama, 'tis no matter how absurdly things
are brought about——So——you Rabble there——
run and cry, A Reprieve!——let the Prisoner be
brought back to his Wives in Triumph.

Player. All this we must do, to comply with the
Taste of the Town.

Beggar. Through the whole Piece you may ob-
serve such a Similitude of Manners in high and low
Life, that it is difficult to determine whether (in the
fashionable Vices) the fine Gentlemen imitate the
Gentlemen of the Road, or the Gentlemen of the
Road the fine Gentlemen.——Had the Play remained, as I at first intended, it would have carried
a most excellent Moral. 'Twould have shown that

PICTORIAL REPRESENTATION OF BEGGAR'S OPERA
OF CONTEMPORARY DATE

the lower Sort of People have their Vices in a degree as well as the Rich : And that they are punish'd for them.

SCENE XVII.

To them, MACHEATH with Rabble, &c.

Macheath. So, it seems, I am not left to my Choice, but must have a Wife at last.——Look ye, my Dears, we will have no Controversy now. Let us give this Day to Mirth, and I am sure she who thinks herself my Wife will testify her Joy by a Dance.

All. Come, a Dance——a Dance.

Macheath. Ladies, I hope you will give me leave to present a Partner to each of you. And (if I may without Offence) for this time, I take *Polly* for mine. ——And for Life, you Slut,——for we were really marry'd.——As for the rest.——But at present keep your own Secret.   [*To* Polly.

A DANCE.

AIR LXIX.—Lumps of Pudding, &c.

Thus I stand like the Turk, *with his Doxies around;*
From all Sides their Glances his Passion confound;
For Black, Brown and Fair, his Inconstancy burns,
And the different Beauties subdue him by turns:

Each calls forth her Charms, to provoke his Desires;
Though willing to all, with but one he retires.
But think of this Maxim, and put off your Sorrow,
The Wretch of To-day, may be happy To-morrow.

CHORUS. *But think of this Maxim, &c.*

FINIS.

MRS. CROUCH AS POLLY

NOTES

Page 1. *Through all the Employments of Life, etc.*

'Some of those songs that contained the severest satire against the Court were written by Pope; particularly,

"Thro' all the Employments of Life,"

and also,

"Since Laws were made," etc.' (See p. 89.)

(Pope's *Works*, ed. Warton, etc., 1797, IX, 99 *n*.)

'What can be prettier than Gay's ballad, or rather Swift's, Arbuthnot's, Pope's and Gay's, in the *What d'ye Call It?*—"'Twas when the seas were roaring"? I have been well informed that they all contributed, and that the most celebrated association of clever fellows this country ever saw did not think it beneath them to unite their strength and abilities in the composition of a song. The success, however, answered to their wishes, and our puny days will never produce such another' (*Correspondence of William Cowper*, ed. Thomas Wright, 4 vols., 1904, II, 92. *Cf.* Spence's *Anecdotes*, 1858, p. 264).

'Dr. Arbuthnot was the sole writer of *John Bull*; and so was Gay of *The Beggar's Opera*.'—POPE. (Spence's *Anecdotes*, ed. Singer, pp. 109-110.)

'We now and then gave a correction, or a word or two of advice: but it was wholly of his own writing.'—POPE. (*Ibid.*, p. 120.) See above, Appendix to Introduction, p. xxix.

'Whereas the airs in *The Beggar's Opera*, many of which are very soft, never fail to render me gay, because they are associated with the warm sensations and high spirits of London' (Boswell's *Life of Johnson*, ed. Hill, III, 198).

'Arbuthnot's daughter, Anne, is said to have furnished Gay with the airs for *The Beggar's Opera*, which are all Scotch. This story rests upon the testimony of Mr. Robert Arbuthnot, Secretary to the Board of Trustees, Edinburgh, who was intimately acquainted with Anne's brother, George' (*The Life and Works of John Arbuthnot*, by George A. Aitken, Oxford, 1892, p. 120, note 1).

'The Duchess of Queensberry told Dr. Warton "that Gay could play on the flute, and that this enabled him to adapt so happily some airs"' (Pope's *Works*, ed. Warton, 1822, I, 203; quoted in Johnson's *Lives of the Poets*, ed. Hill, II, 276, note 3).

'Gay could play on the flute, and was therefore enabled to adapt so happily some of the airs in *The Beggar's Opera*' (Spence's *Anecdotes*, ed. Singer, p. 237 *n*.).

Page 5. *Robin of Bagshot, etc.*

'The intended affront was plain to all the world. Nobody could doubt that Robin of Bagshot, alias bluff Bob, alias Carbuncle, alias Bob Booty, was design'd to typify, by his various names, Sir Robert's unrefined manners, convivial habits, and alleged robbery of the public. His system of bribery was pointedly attacked, and Macheath was provided with both a wife and a mistress to indicate that Lady Walpole had a rival in Miss Skerrett ' (Pope's *Works*, ed. Elwin and Courthope, VII, 117, note 1).

Page 11. *Hockley in the Hole.*

'Boswell, I believe, is coming. He talks of being here to-day. I shall be glad to see him. But he shrinks from the Baltick expedition, which I think is the best scheme in our power. What we shall substitute, I know not. He wants to see Wales, but except the woods of Bachycraigh what is there in Wales ? What can fill the hunger of ignorance, or quench the thirst of curiosity ? We may perhaps form some scheme or other, but, in the phrase of Hockley in the Hole, it is a pity he has not a better bottom.'—Johnson to Mrs. Thrale, Sept. 13, 1777 (*Letters of Samuel Johnson*, ed. Hill, 2 vols., Oxford, 1892, II, 30).

['The want of what in the language of boxers is termed *bottom* on the part of the combatants disgusted the company exceedingly.']—*Sporting Magazine*, April, 1796, p. 46.

The *Spectator* describes Hockley in the Hole, in Clerkenwell, as : 'a place of no small renown for the gallantry of the lower order of Britons ' (No. 436).

'Jonathan married Elizabeth, daughter of Scragg Hollow, of Hockley in the Hole, Esq., and by her had Jonathan, who is the illustrious subject of these memoirs.'—Fielding's *Jonathan Wild*, bk. I, ch. ii. (See Boswell's *Life of Johnson*, ed. Hill, III, 134, note 1.)

Page 14. *As Men should serve a Cowcumber, etc.*

'Gay, during his whole life, was remarkably subject to complaints arising from indigestion, and 'tis probable that under the influence of this suffering, he composed the two latter lines of the song in *The Beggar's Opera*, where Mrs. Peachum, complaining of her daughter's taste for finery, says :

" And when she's dress'd with care and cost,
    All tempting fine and gay,
As men should serve a cucumber,
    She flings herself away." '

(Ballard's Memoir in *Gay's Chair*, ed. Henry Lee, London, 1820, p. 21 *n*.) [The Rev. Joseph Ballard was Gay's nephew.]

'By the by, Dr. Johnson told me, that Gay's line in *The Beggar's Opera*, " As men should serve a cucumber," etc., has no waggish meaning, with reference to men flinging away cucumbers as too *cooling*, which some have thought ; for it has been a common saying of physicians in England, that a cucumber should be well sliced, and dressed with pepper and vinegar, and then thrown out, as good for nothing ' (Boswell's *Life of Johnson*, ed. Hill, V, 289).

Page 22. *O ponder well ! etc.*

'And indeed, it [*The Beggar's Opera*] had like to have miscarried and been damned, till Polly sung in a most tender and affecting manner, the words

" For on the rope that hangs my dear
    Depends poor Polly's life."

This is the Air that is said irresistibly to have conquered the Lover who afterwards married her ' (Pope's *Works*, ed. Warton, 1797, IX, 100 *n*.).

Page 29. *Jemmy Twitcher.*

This title was afterwards given to the Earl of Sandwich who, by bribing the printers, procured a copy of Wilkes's immoral *Essay on Woman*, and laid it on the table of the House of Lords, thereby involving Wilkes in a duel and subsequent flight to France. The incident is described by Macaulay, who adds:

'In the minds even of many moral and religious men his [Wilkes's] crime seemed light when compared with the crime of his accusers. The conduct of Sandwich, in particular, excited universal disgust. His own vices were notorious; and, only a fortnight before he laid the *Essay on Woman* before the House of Lords, he had been drinking and singing loose catches with Wilkes at one of the most dissolute clubs in London. Shortly after the meeting of Parliament, *The Beggar's Opera* was acted at Covent Garden theatre. When Macheath uttered the words—"That Jemmy Twitcher should peach me I own surprised me"— pit, boxes, and galleries, burst into a roar which seemed likely to bring the roof down. From that day Sandwich was universally known by the nickname of Jemmy Twitcher' (Macaulay's *Essays*, Popular Edn., 1906, pp. 769-70 [*The Earl of Chatham*]).

'This evening's party was closed by the entrance of the Earl of Sandwich, of famous name and character.

'I thought of *Jemmy Twitcher* immediately. He is a tall, stout man, and looks as weather proof as any sailor in the navy. He has great good-humour and joviality marked in his countenance' (*Early Diary of Frances Burney*, ed. A. R. Ellis, 2 vols., 1889, II, 125).

For Gray's verses on him, see *The Works of Thomas Gray*, ed. E. Gosse, 4 vols., 1884, I, 131-2; also *Poetical Works of Gray and Collins*, ed. Austin Lane Poole, Oxford, 1917, p. 109.

Page 30. *Practical philosophers.*

'If a man firmly believes that religion is an invaluable treasure, he will consider a writer who endeavours to deprive mankind of it as a *robber*; he will look upon him as *odious*, though the infidel might think himself in the right. A robber who reasons as the gang do in *The Beggar's Opera*, who call themselves *practical* philosophers, and may have as much sincerity as pernicious *speculative* philosophers, is not the less an object of just indignation' (Boswell's *Life of Johnson*, ed. Hill, II, 442).

Page 48. *Scene X.*

'I did not understand that the scene of Lockit and Peachum's quarrel was an imitation of one between Brutus and Cassius till I was told it. I wish Macheath, when he was going to be hanged, had imitated Alexander the Great when he was dying. I would have had his fellow-rogues desire his commands about a successor, and he to answer, "Let it be the most worthy," etc.'—Swift to Gay, March 28, 1728 (Swift's *Correspondence*, IV, 20. *Cf.* Shakespeare's *Julius Caesar*, IV, 3).

Coxe records how in 1729 Walpole 'met Townshend at Colonel Selwyn's, in Cleveland Court, in the presence of the Duke of Newcastle, Mr. Pelham, Colonel and Mrs. Selwyn. The conversation turned on a foreign negotiation, which at the desire of Walpole had been relinquished. Townshend, however, still required that the measure should be mentioned to the Commons, at the same time that the House should be informed that it was given up. Walpole objecting to this proposal as inexpedient, and calculated only to give unnecessary trouble, Townshend said, "Since you object, and the House of Commons is your concern more than mine, I shall not persist in my opinion; but as I now give way, I cannot avoid observing, that upon my honour I think that mode of proceeding would have been most advisable." Walpole, piqued at these expressions, lost his temper, and said, " My lord, for once, there is no man's sincerity which I doubt so much as your lordship's, and I never doubted it so much as when you are pleased to make such strong professions." Townshend, incensed at this reproach, seized him by the collar, Sir Robert laid hold of him in return, and then both, at the same instant, quitted their hold, and laid their hands upon their swords. Mrs. Selwyn, alarmed, attempted to go out and call the guards, but was prevented by Pelham. But although their friends interposed to prevent an immediate duel, yet the contumelious expressions used on this occasion, rendered all attempts to heal the breach ineffectual' (Coxe's *Memoirs of Sir Robert Walpole*, I, 335-6).

In a note to Hervey's story of a dispute between Lord Townshend and Sir Robert Walpole, Croker remarks : 'It is odd that Lord Hervey should not allude (if it had ever happened) to the much more remarkable altercation and *personal scuffle* between Walpole and Townshend, said to have occurred at Mrs. Selwyn's in Cleveland Court, and supposed to have been the original of the celebrated quarrel scene between Peachum and Lockit in *The Beggar's Opera*. Coxe, who (as far as I know) first told the story, does not *specify* his authority, and dates it in 1729. Lord Mahon repeats it, but assigns no authority, and places it under the date of 1730, just before Townshend's resignation. This would seem the more probable, as after such a scene it is hard to imagine the parties could have continued to sit in the same Cabinet; but as *The Beggar's Opera* was played on the 29th January 1728, it is certain either that the date of the historians is an anachronism, or that Gay alluded to some earlier dispute, or that the story was made from the scene' (Hervey's *Memoirs*, ed. Croker, 1884, I, 117 *n*.).

'Many persons have imagined that the scene in which Peachum and Lockit first reproached, and then collared one another, was a satire on a similar fray between Walpole and Lord Townshend. This interpretation would add zest to both action and dialogue. But the notion is not countenanced by Swift's expressions, and is inconsistent with Lord Hervey's testimony that the quarrels of the two ministers had not publicly transpired when *The Beggar's Opera* was produced, and with Coxe's statement that the scuffle, which was the climax, did not occur till 1729' (Pope's *Works*, ed. Elwin and Courthope, VII, 125, note 3).

' Besides the general reflections on courts and courtiers, it is well known that the quarrelling scene between Peachum and Lockit was written in express ridicule of certain disputes among the ministers of the day, and accordingly excited the most ungovernable mirth among the audience' (Swift's *Works*, ed. Scott, 1824, IX, 94 *n*.).

Page 49. *When you censure the Age*, etc.
See Introduction, p. xvii, and note 5.

Page 84. *But two at a time there's no mortal can bear*.
' Some time after this, upon his [Johnson's] making a remark which escaped my attention, Mrs. Williams and Mrs. Hall were both together striving to answer him. He grew angry, and called out loudly, "Nay, when you both speak at once, it is intolerable." But checking himself, and softening, he said, " This one

may say, though you *are* ladies." Then he brightened into gay humour, and addressed them in the words of one of the songs of *The Beggar's Opera*:

> But two at a time there's no mortal can bear.

"What, Sir, (said I,) are you going to turn Captain Macheath?" There was something so pleasantly ludicrous in this scene as can be imagined. The contrast between Macheath, Polly, and Lucy—and Dr. Samuel Johnson, blind, peevish Mrs. Williams, and lean, lank, preaching Mrs. Hall, was exquisite' (Boswell's *Life of Johnson*, ed. Hill, IV, 95).

Page 89. *Since Laws were made, etc.*
   Pope has expressed the same idea in the lines:

> ' The thief damns judges, and the knaves of state,
> And dying mourns small villains hanged by great.'

The couplet occurs in some MS. lines inserted in the *Essay on Man*, Epistle II, after line 226. (See Pope's *Works*, ed. Elwin and Courthope, II, 393-4, note 4.)

SUPPLEMENT

The Music for the Overture and the Songs in The Beggar's Opera,
Reproduced from the Original 1729 Edition

OUVERTURE in SCORE

Compos'd by Dr. *PEPUSCH.*

A

The OUVERTURE.

the Repeat pia:

The O U V E R T U R E.

Solo
Solo
Piano
Piano

tutti
tutti
forte
forte

SONGS in the BEGGAR's OPERA.

ACT I.

AIR I. An old woman cloathed in gray.

Thro' all the employments of life. Each neighbour a-bu-ſes his brother; Whore and Rogue they call Huſband and Wife: All profeſſions be-rogue one a-nother. The Prieſt calls the Lawyer a cheat, The Lawyer beknaves the Di-vine. And the Stateſman, becauſe he's ſo great, Thinks his trade as honeſt as mine.

AIR II. The bonny gray-ey'd morn. &c.

'Tis Woman that ſe-duces all mankind, By her we firſt were taught the

B

wheedling Arts: Her very eyes can cheat; when most she's kind, She tricks us

of our money with our hearts. For her like Wolves by night we roam for prey, And

practise ev'ry fraud to bribe her charms; For suits of Love, like Law, are

won by pay, And beauty must be fee'd into our arms.

AIR III. Cold and raw, &c.

If any wench Venus's girdle wear, Though she be never so ugly;

Lillies and roses will quickly appear, And her face look wond'rous smuggly. Be=

=neath the left ear so fit but a cord, (A rope so charming a Zone is!) The

AIR IV. Why is your faithful slave disdain'd?

AIR V. Of all the simple things we do.

here, now there; is bought, or is sold; And is current in every house.

AIR VI. What shall I do to shew how much I love her.

Virgins are like the fair flow'r in its lustre, Which in the garden e=

=namels the ground; Near it the Bees in play flutter & cluster, & gaudy Butterflies

frolick around. But, when once pluckt, 'tis no longer al=luring, to Covent=

=Garden 'tis sent, (as yet sweet,) There fades, and shrinks and grows

past all en=during, Rots, stinks, & dies, & is trod under feet.

AIR VII. Oh London is a fine town.

Our Polly is a sad slut! nor heeds what we have taught her. I wonder any

thought it both safest and best To marry, for fear you should chide.

AIR IX. *O Jenny, O Jenny, where hast thou been?*

O Polly, you might have toy'd and kist. By keeping men off, you keep them on.

But he so teaz'd me, And he so pleas'd me, What I did, you must have done.

AIR X. *Thomas, I cannot, &c.*

I, like a Ship in storms, was tost; Yet afraid to put in to land; For

seiz'd in the port the vessel's lost, Whose treasure is contreband. The

waves are laid, My du-ty's paid. O Joy beyond Expres=sion! Thus safe ashore, I

ask no more, My all is in my possession, possession, My all is in my possession.

AIR XI. A soldier and a sailor

A fox may steal your hens, Sir, A whore your health and pence, Sir, Your

daughter rob your chest, Sir, Your wife may steal your rest, Sir, A thief your goods and

Plate. A Thief your Goods & Plate. But this is

all but Picking, With rest, pence, chest & chicken; It e = ver

was decreed, Sir, If Law = yer's hand is feed Sir, he Steals your whole Es =

:tate. he Steals your whole Estate

AIR XII. Now ponder well, ye parents dear.

Oh, ponder well! be not severe; So save a wretched

wife! For on the rope that hangs my Dear, depends poor Polly's life.

AIR XIII. Le printemps rappelle aux armes.

The Turtle thus with Plaintive crying, her lover = dying,

The Turtle thus with Plaintive crying, La = ments her Dove. Down she

drops quite Spent with Sighing, Pair'd in death, as = pair'd in Love.

AIR XIV. Pretty Parrot, say.

Pretty Polly, say, When I was away, Did your fancy never

stray to some newer Lo = ver? Without Disguise, = Heaving

Sighs, = Doating Eyes, My constant heart discover. Fond =

on my charmer's breaſt repos'd. And I would love you all the day, Every night would

kiſs and play. If with me you'd fondly ſtray Over the hills and far away.

AIR XVII. Gin thou wert mine awn thing.

O what pain it is to part! Can I leave thee, can I leave thee?

O what pain it is to part! Can thy Polly ever leave thee?

But leſt death my love ſhoud thwart, & bring thee to the fa=tal Cart, Thus I

tear thee from my bleeding heart! Fly hence, & let me leave thee

AIR XVIII. O the broom, &c.

The Miſer thus a ſhilling ſees, Which he's oblig'd to pay, With

sighs resigns it by degrees, And fears 'tis gone for aye. The Boy, tho'when his

Sparrow's flown, The bird in silence eyes; But soon as out of

sight 'tis gone, Whines, whimpers, sobs and cries.

End of the First Act.

A C T II.

AIR XIX. Fill ev'ry glass &c

Fill e'ry glass, for Wine inspires us, And fires us, With courage, love &

joy. Women and wine should life employ. Is there ought else on earth de-si--rous

Da Cap.

AIR XX. March in *Rinaldo*, with drums and trumpets

Let us take the road. Hark! I hear the sound of coaches! The

hour of attack approaches! To your arms brave boys and load. See the Ball I

hold! Let the Chymists toil like asses Our fire their fire sur-

-passes. And turns all our lead to gold.

AIR XXI. Wou'd you have a young Virgin, &c.

If the heart of a man is deprest with cares, The mist is dispell'd when a woman appears; Like the notes of a fiddle, she sweetly, sweetly Raises the spirits and charms our ears. Roses and lillies her cheeks disclose But her ripe lips are more sweet than those. Press her, Caress her With blisses her kisses dis= =solve us in pleasure, and soft repose

AIR XXII. Cotillon

Youth's the season made for joys, Love is then our Duty; She alone who that employs, Well deserves her beauty, Let's be gay, While we may, Beauty's a

flower despis'd in decay. Youth's the Season made for Joys, Love is then our

duty. Let us drink and sport to-day, Ours is not to-morrow. Love with Youth flies

swift away, Age is nought but Sorrow. Dance and sing, Time's on the wing, Life never

knows the return of Spring. Let us drink and sport to day, Ours is not to-morrow.

AIR XXIII. All in a misty morning, &c.

Before the barn-door crowing, the Cock by Hens attended, His eyes around him

throwing, Stands for a while suspended. Then one he singles from the crew, and

cheers the happy Hen; With how d'you do, and how d'you do, And how d'you do again.

AIR XXIV.   When once I lay with another man's wife.

The Gamesters and Lanyers are jugglers alike, If they meddle your all is in

danger. Like Gypsies, if once they can finger a souse, Your pockets they pick, and they

pilfer your house, And give your estate to a stranger.

AIR XXV.   When first I laid siege to my *Chloris*.

At the Tree I shall suffer with pleasure: Let me go where I will, In

all kinds of ill, I shall find no such Furies as these are.

AIR XXVI.   Courtiers, Courtiers, think it no harm.

Man may escape from rope and gun;   Nay, some have out-liv'd the

Doctor's pill: Who takes a woman must be undone, that Basi= lisk is

sure to kill. The Fly that sips Treacle is lost in the sweets, so

he that tastes Woman, Woman, Woman, he that tastes Woman, ruin meets.

AIR XXVII. A lovely lass to a Friar came.

Thus when a good huswife sees a Rat in her trap in the morning taken,

With pleasure her heart goes pit a pat, In revenge for her loss of bacon. Then she

throws him To the Dog or Cat, To be worried, crush'd and shaken.

AIR XXVIII. 'Twas when the Sea was roaring.

How cruel are the traytors, Who lye and swear in jest, To cheat un=

=guarded creatures Of virtue, fame, and rest! Whoever steals a shilling, Thro'

shame the guilt conceals: In love the perjur'd villain With boasts the theft reveals.

AIR XXIX. The Sun had loos'd his weary teams.

The first time at the lookingglass The mother sets her daughter: The

Image strikes the smiling lass With self-love ever after. Each

time she looks, she, fonder grown, Thinks ev'ry charm grows stronger: But a-

las, vain maid, all eyes but your own Can see you are not younger.

AIR XXX. How happy are we, &c.

When you censure the age, Be cautious and sage, Lest the Courtiers of-

= fended shou'd be: If you mention Vice or bribe, 'Tis so

D

pat to all the Tribe each crys that was levell'd at me.

AIR XXXI. Of a noble race was *Shenkin.*

Is then his fate decreed Sir? - - - -

Such a Man can I think of quitting? When

first we met so moves me yet, O see how my heart is splitting!

AIR XXXII.

You'll think, e'er many days ensue, This sentence not severe; I hang your

husband, child, 'tis true, But with him hang your care. Twang dang dillo dee.

AIR XXXIII. *London* Ladies.

If you at an Office solicit your due, And would not have matters neg=

:lected: You must quicken the Clerk with the perquisite too, To

do what his duty direc=ted. Or would you the frowns of a

lady prevent, She too has this palpable failing. The

perquisite softens her into consent; that reason with all is prevailing.

AIR XXXIV. All in the Downs, &c.

Thus when the Swallow, seeking prey, Within the sash is closely

pent, His consort with bemoaning lay, Without sits pining for th' event.

Her chatt'ring lovers all around her skim; She heeds them not (poor bird) her soul's w.th him.

D. 2.

By their flirting Women oft have envy shown: Pleas'd, to ruin Others wooing:

Never happy in their own,

AIR XXXVIII. *Good morow, Goſsip Joan.*

Why how now, Madam Flirt, If ---- you this must chatter;

And are for finging Dir ------------------------------------ t, Let's

try who best can fput ---- ter; Madam Flirt. Why how now, Saucy

Jade! Sure the Wench is Tipsey. How can you see me made=

============== = The ſcoff of ſuch a Gip = ſey? Saucy Jade!

AIR XXX . How happy are , &c .

No power on earth can e'er divide, The knot that sacred Love hath ty'd.

When parents draw against our mind, The true-love's knot they faster bind, Ho hora in

ambo = ra =   ho   an ho derry hi   an hi derry

hoo hoo derry   derry   derry Derry   ambo = ra - - - -

AIR XL . The Lass of Patie's Mill, &c.

I like the Fox shall grieve, Whose mate hath left her side, Whom

Hounds, from morn to eve, Chase o'er the country wide. Where can my lover

hide? Where cheat the wary pack? If Love be not his guide, He never will come back!

End of the Second Act.

ACT III.

AIR XLI. If Love's a sweet passion &c.

When young at the bar you first taught me to score, And bid me be free of my lips, and no more; I was kiss'd by the Parson, the Squire, and the Sot: When the guest was departed, the kiss was forgot. But his kiss was so sweet, and so closely he prest, That I languish'd and pin'd 'till I granted the rest.

AIR XLII. South Sea Ballad.

My love is all madness and folly, alone I lye, toss, tumble and cry, What a happy creature is Polly! — Was e'er such a wretch as

I - - With rage I redden like Scarlet, = That my dear in =

= con = stant Varlet= Stark blind to my charms, is lost in the

arms Of that Jilt; that inveigling) Harlot! Stark blind to my charms, is

lost in the arms Of that Jilt, that inveigling) Harlot! This, this my re =

= sentiment alarms.

AIR XLIII. Packington's Pound.

Thus Gamesters united in friendship are found, Though they know that their

industry all is a cheat; They flock to their prey at the Dice box's Sound, And

join to promote one another's deceit. But if by mishap They fail of a chap; To

keep in their hands, they each other entrap. Like Pikes, lank with hunger. who

miss of their ends, They bite their companions, and prey on their friends.

AIR XLIV. Lillibulero.

The modes of the Court so common are grown, That a true friend can

hardly be met; Friendship for interest is but a loan, Which they let out for

what they can get; 'Tis true, you find Some friends so kind, Who'll give you good

counsel themselves to defend. In sorrowful ditty, They promise, they

E

pity, But shift you for money, from friend to friend.

AIR XLV. Down in the North Country.

What Gudgeons are we Men, Evry Woman's easy Prey, Tho' we have felt the

Hook, agen = — We bite and they betray. The Bird that has been

trapt, when he hears his calling Mate: To her he flies, a=gain he's

clapt = = within the Wiry Grate:

AIR XLVI. A Shepherd kept sheep, &c.

In the Days of my youth I cou'd bill like a Dove fa la la

fa &c. In the days of my youth I cou'd bill like a Dove, Like a

Sparrow at all times was ready for Love.

The life of all Mortals in kissing should pass,

The life of all Mortals in kissing should pass, Lip to

lip while you're young, then the lip to the Glass.

AIR XLVII. One evening having lost my way.

I'm like a Ship on the Ocean tost, Now high, now low, with each Billow

born, With her rudder broke and her anchor lost, De-sert-ed and all for=

lorn, While thus I lye rolling and tossing all Night, That Polley lyes

Sporting on Seas of Delight; Revenge, revenge, revenge, shall ap————

————pease my restless Sprite.

AIR XLVIII. Now *Roger*, I'll tell thee, because thou'rt my Son.

When a wife's in her pout, as she's sometimes no doubt; The good

husband as meek as a lamb, Her vapours to still, first grants her her will, & the

quieting draught is a dram, Poor man! and the quieting draught is a dram.

AIR XLIX. O *Bessy Bell* &c.

A curse attends that woman's love, Who always would be pleasing. The

pertness of the billing Dove, Like tickling is but teazing, What then in love can

woman do? If we grow fond they shun us, And when we fly them,

they pursue; But leave us when they're won us.

AIR L. Wou'd Fate to me *Belinda* give.

Among the men, Coquets we find, Who court by turns all Wo=man=

=kind; And we grant all their hearts desir'd, When they are flatter'd,

when they are flatter'd, when they are flatter'd, and admir'd.

AIR LI, Come, sweet lass

Come sweet lass, Lets banish sorrow, Till to morrow: Come, sweet lass, Lets

tahe a chirping Glass, Wine can clear the vapours of despair; And make us light as

air; then drink and ba .. nish care.

AIR LII. The last time I went o'er the Moor.

Hither dear husband, turn your eyes Bestow one glance to cheer me, Think

with that look thy Polly dyes, O shun me not but hear me. Tis Polly sues, Tis

Lu...cy speaks. Is thus true love requit ed? My heart is bursting. Mine too

breaks, Must I, must I be Slight= = ed.

AIR LIII. Tom Tinker's my true love &c.

Which way shall I turn me, how can I decide? Wives the day of our

Death are as fond as a Bride: One Wife is too much for most husbands to

hear; but two at a time there's no Mortal can bear. This way, and

that way, and which way I will, What wou'd comfort the one t'other wife wou'd take ill.

AIR LIV. I am a poor Shepherd undone.

When my hero in court appears, And stands arraign'd for his life; Then

think of poor Polly's tears; For ah! Poor Polly's his wife. Like the Sailor he

holds up his hand, Distrest on the dashing wave. To die a dry death at land, Is as

bad as a watry grave. And alas, poor Polly! Alack, and well-a-day! Before I

was in love. Oh! every month was May.

AIR LV. _Ianthe the lovely, &c._

When he holds up his hand arraign'd for his life, O think of your

daughter, and think I'm his wife! What are cannons, or bombs, or clashing of

swords? For death is more certain by witnesses words. Then nail up their lips; that dread

thunder allay; And each month of my life, And each month of my life will here=

=after be May.

AIR LVI. _A Cobler there was, &c._

Ourselves, like the great, to secure a retreat, When matters re=

equire it, must give up our gang: And good reason why, Or, instead of the fry, Ev'n

Peachum and I, Like poor petty rascals, might hang, hang; Like

poor petty rascals, might hang.

AIR LVII. Bonny Dundee.

The charge is prepar'd; the Lawyers are met; The Judges all rang'd (a

terrible show!) I go, undismay'd. For death is a debt, A debt on demand. So,

take what I owe. Then farewell, my love; dear charmers, adieu. Contented I die 'tis the

better for you. Here ends all dispute the rest of our lives. For this way at

once I please all my wives.

AIR LVIII. Happy Groves.

O cruel, cruel, cruel case! Must I suffer this disgrace?

AIR LIX. Of all the girls that are so smart.

Of all the friends in time of grief, When threatning death looks grimmer;-

Not one so sure can bring relief, As this best friend a brimmer.

AIR LX. Britons strike Home.

Since I must swing, --I scorn, I scorn to wince or whine.

AIR LXI. Chevy Chase.

But now again my spirits sink, I'll raise them high with   wine.

AIR LXII. To old Sir Simon the King.

But valour the stronger grows, The stronger liquor we're drinking. And

how can we feel our woes, When we've lost the trouble of thinking?

AIR LXIII. Joy to great *Cæsar.*

If thus A man can die Much bolder with brandy.

AIR LXIV. There was an old woman, &c.

So I drink off this bumper And now I can stand the test: And my

Comrades shall see, that I die as brave as the best.

AIR LXV. Did you ever hear of a gallant sailor.

But can I leave my pretty hussies, without one tear, or tender sigh?

AIR LXVI. Why are mine eyes still flowing.

Their eyes, their lips, their Bus = = = ses recall my love. Ah

must I die!

AIR LXVII.   Green ſleeves.

Since laws were made for ev'ry degree, To curb vice in others, as

well as me, I wonder we han't better company, Upon Ty - - burn Tree!

But Gold from law can take out the Sting; And if rich men like us were to

swing, 'Twou'd thin the land, such Numbers to string upon Ty - - burn Tree!

AIR LXVIII.   All you that muſt take a leap, &c.

Would I might be hang'd! And I would ſo too! To be hang'd with

you, My dear, with you, O leave me to thought! I fear! I doubt! I tremble! I

droop! See, my courage is out. No token of love? See my courage is out. No token of

AIR LXIX. Lumps of Pudding, &c.

willing to all; with but one he retires. But think of this Maxim, and

put off all Sorrow, The Wretch of to day, may be happy to morrow.

Each calls forth her charms, to pro =

= voke his desires. Tho' willing to all, with but one he retires. - But

think of this Maxim, and put off all Sorrow, The wretch of to day, may be

happy to Morrow.

FINIS.